THE
RUSSIAN
IMPERIAL CONSPIRACY
1892 - 1914

OWEN

THE
RUSSIAN IMPERIAL
CONSPIRACY

1892-1914

BY

ROBERT L. OWEN

~~~~~~~~~

NEW YORK
ALBERT AND CHARLES BONI
1927

DEDICATION

To the Fathers and Mothers and to the youth of
France and of Germany, and of the World; to all
lovers of truth and fair play

THIS VOLUME IS DEDICATED

With the friendly suggestion that

A GLORIOUS LIFE IN PEACE

IS

BETTER

THAN

A GLORIOUS DEATH IN BATTLE

THE RUSSIAN IMPERIAL CONSPIRACY OF 1892-1914

THE MOST GIGANTIC INTRIGUE OF ALL TIME

The Germans did not will the war. It was forced on them by the Russian Imperialists—Grand Duke Nicholas, Isvolski, Sazonoff, Sukhomlinoff, and associates in control of Russia. The German, Russian, French, Belgian and allied peoples became alike the sorrowful victims.

RECENT EVIDENCE

of the INNER SECRETS OF EUROPEAN DIPLOMACY proves this.

An effort so to condense the vital evidence that a busy man may conveniently read it.

The happiness and future peace of the world require the reconciliation of the German and French people.

FOREWORD

In the summer of 1923 in Europe there fell into my hands at Paris the work of René Marchand—*Un Livre Noir*—containing the secret dispatches between the Russian Foreign Office and Isvolski, the Ambassador of Russia at Paris immediately preceding the World War.

In London I obtained de Sieberts' publication of the like secret dispatches between the Russian Foreign Office and Benckendorf, the Ambassador of Russia at London.

My interest was thus aroused and every book available on the subject was studied because it was perceived that the Allied Propaganda that they had fought unselfishly for democratic principles and to establish justice and right in international affairs had greatly deceived the people of the United States.

It became perfectly obvious that the theory that the Czar was leading the fight to make the world safe for Democracy was ludicrous.

These Secret Dispatches showed that the theory that the war was waged in defense of American ideals was untrue.

They also proved that the theory that the Entente Allies were fighting a war to defend themselves and the United States from the criminal design of William II to dominate the world by military force was false.

It became clear that a few leaders of the Entente Allies had instigated and launched the war inspired by the mixed motives of imperialistic ambitions, greed for commercial and political power, future security, revenge, hate, love of secret diplomacy and intrigue, believing that the war would be quickly ended, that the profit would be great and the future enjoyment of such illicit gains well protected.

When the Records had been studied, the evidence and my conclusions were presented to the American People in the United States Senate, December 18, 1923. My action was moved alone by my love for the people of the United States, feeling that it was my duty as a matter of loyalty, to disclose to them the truth, even if I seemed quite alone.

Now that European interests are vigorously declaring by a second great American Propaganda that it was *"Our War,"* as a basis for cancelling the War Debts, it has seemed worth while to put in a compact form the evidence to show it was not "Our War," and to show the Common People of all the nations that they have been the victims of imperial intrigue and unwise leadership, and that they should, by democratic processes, defend themselves in future against the secret diplomacy and intrigue of unintelligent officials.—R. L. O.

TABLE OF CONTENTS

THE
RUSSIAN
IMPERIAL CONSPIRACY

CHAPTER I

INTRODUCTION

I. The Problem

The most gigantic conspiracy of all time in its consequences was the intrigue of the Russian Imperialists, who deliberately and intentionally brought about the World War in 1914. Isvolski was the evil genius chiefly responsible for the final explosion.

The object was the control of Constantinople and the Dardanelles, over-lordship in the Balkans and the seizure of German and Austrian territory.

The motive was imperial greed for power, political, commercial and financial.

The German territory lay between Russian and French territory with no adequate natural defensive boundaries. The German theory was that they must be strong enough to prevent successful attack by Russia and France. The German leaders prepared against war and greatly feared it. They knew the terrible odds against them. They hoped their preparedness would keep the Russian leaders from attacking. Their hopes proved to be vain.

An intimate study of the causes of the World War and its

results shows that *the common peoples* of Europe did not will aggressive war; that they were patriotic, brave and determined to defend their own homes, but they did not have the will to invade their neighbors' territory for profit. The people of the belligerent nations were trained in the art of war and made to believe it a virtue to cultivate the spirit of a soldier. Militarism was common to all.

All the people involved were, probably 90 per cent. or more, innocent of wrong purposes, and they were all, whether victorious or defeated, the victims of this tragedy.

Over thirty-seven million people suffered death or mutilation, and other unrecorded millions disappeared. Six million died from civil strife and forty million from consequent epidemics; hundreds of millions suffered indescribable sorrows and anxiety. It was through no conscious fault of their own. They merit compassion.

Whenever the people realize the great truth that they were misled, that they were deceived by propaganda, that they were all alike victims of the errors of unwise leadership, it may be possible for them to understand each other and to feel sympathy rather than hate, and understanding and good will may be established.

Imperialists profited by international hate and promoted it. They taught autocracy was necessary for war defense and that the safety of the people required intensive military preparation and centralized power.

The German Kaiser occasionally rattled the sword and cultivated militarism while declaring himself the guardian of peace. The czar built up a huge army. Austria, Serbia, France, Italy, developed their arms to the extent of their taxing power.

The people all went to the battlefields of death with courage and loyalty, praying to God to bless the cause for which they were making the supreme sacrifice. The history of their sufferings is the history of their credulity and patriotism. The spirit of excessive nationalism, militarism and imperialism built up through centuries, was the atmosphere which made this war possible, but the deliberate plans of the Russian Imperial conspirators, who clearly saw the possibility, made it a certainty. The Russian Foreign Office leaders willed and planned the war, and unhappily found in the ambition of the Serbian leaders and in the fears, hates and ambitions of a very few French leaders the material which made the conspiracy brilliantly successful, as an intrigue, but a hideous and ghastly tragedy in the final issues.

It is doubtful if one Frenchman in ten thousand had any knowledge that Poincaré was deliberately leading France to war. Neither the Russian nor French government really believed that the German government intended aggressive war on them but the military preparedness of Germany and the bombast of some of its chauvinists laid a convenient but false foundation for the French and British propaganda that the German leaders had plotted the brutal military conquest of the world.

The reconciliation of the French and German people, their mutual heartfelt moral disarmament is essential to physical disarmament; their mutual respect and good-will are vital to their future peace and the future peace of Europe and the world.

Valliant Coutourier, member of the French House of Delegates, in accusing Raymond Poincaré of having been responsible with the Russian leaders for having caused the war, did so "on his honor as an old French soldier"; and so "on my honor as a long-time member of the United States Senate," I record the accusing evidence in this book and my profound conviction that the conclusions are absolutely sound, assuring those who read these lines that they have been written as the result of careful study, entirely free from any conscious prejudice or illwill, even against those believed directly responsible for unloosing the World War, without any desire to stigmatize them, but with the purpose of making the truth known in order that the people may be ultimately reconciled to each other when they can better understand each other.

With this book goes a prayer that it may be of some use in establishing understanding, truth and good will.

R.L.O.

"To sin by silence when we should protest
    Makes cowards out of men.
The few who dare must speak and speak again
    To right the wrongs of men."

"There is no competent and informed historian in any country who has studied the problem of the genesis of the World War in a thorough fashion who does not regard the theory of war guilt held in Articles 227 and 231 in the Versailles Treaty to be wholly false, misleading and unjust." ("Genesis of the War," H. E. Barnes—679.)

"Never before in the whole history of historical writing has there been so rapid and complete a change in the opinions of historians concerning an event of major importance as has been witnessed in the revision of our conceptions concerning the causes of the outbreak of the World War in August, 1914." (ibid. 713.)

II. THE EVIDENCE

The American people are the descendants, almost exclusively, of the European people. Their immediate ancestors are British, German, Scandinavian, Dutch, Russian, French, Italian, Greek, Spanish, etc., but the American people, separated by three thousand miles of water, have been too busy with their own affairs to search out the truth with regard to the origin of the late war. Indeed, the truth itself was completely hidden from sight, first because the archives were profoundly secret, then further obscured by willful falsehood and by a flood of propaganda against the German people, as well as against the German Government. This propaganda was useful to the Entente Powers and their allies. It enabled them to borrow ten billion dollars from the United States, and finally to receive the military and naval aid of the United States, and its powerful financial and commercial support when the German Command conceived it to be necessary as a war measure to submarine American ships.

Fortunately for the world, the overthrow of the absolute monarchy of the Czar of Russia put into the hands of the revolutionary government all of the secret Russian archives which have now been largely published, and from which the world has been able at last to ascertain the actual truth as to the infinitely dangerous intrigues of a few statesmen of Russia, France, Serbia, Great Britain, etc.

With the overthrow of William II the German records were opened wide by the Socialists, who had expected to find the leaders of the German Empire under William, guilty of willing the war. They found their leaders did not will the war.

The seizure of the Belgium records disclosed the secret archives of Belgium.

The overthrow of the monarchy in Austria resulted in a republican government, which made complete exposure or publication of the records of Austria.

In Great Britain under their parliamentary system, important portions of the truth have been made public through parliamentary inquiries and demands, and their Foreign Office records will now be opened to public knowledge. The French records have not been opened, but partly falsified when published.

As a consequence of these extremely important disclosures, the refusals to disclose and falsifications, there no longer remains any reason why the truth should not be known. The truth is known to the historians and scholars of the world. The most important of these secret records is first a book containing 858 secret dispatches passing between the Russian Foreign Office and the Russian Embassy at London, entitled "Entente Diplomacy and the World," by Benno de Siebert (Secretary of the Russian Embassy at London, England), Knickerbocker Press, New York, and "Un Livre Noir", consisting of two volumes edited by René Marchand, published by the Librairie du Travail, Paris, France, containing the secret dispatches between the Russian Foreign Office and Isvolski, Russian Ambassador at Paris. These two records are sufficient completely to disclose the truth with regard to the launching of the World War, and the manner in which it was done. These two books alone contain about 1,500 secret Russian dispatches. Very voluminous quotations from these dispatches will be found in the Congressional Record of December 18, 1923 (pp. 355 to 399). On page 397 (ibid) will be found Exhibit 20, the literature bearing upon this matter, together with a number of books by French and other authors, which justify the conclusions which are set forth in this volume. (See Appendix.)

Among very distinguished French scholars who have pointed out the responsibility of French and Russian leadership for the World War will be found such men as Alfred Fabre-Luce (author of La Victoire), who is a scholar of distinction and a historical author. Victor Margueritte, a distinguished French writer, is responsible for obtaining the first 102 signatures of distinguished French scholars, generals, authors, men and women of Letters, to an appeal to the conscience of France, demanding modification of Article 231, and also the abrogation of Articles 227 to 230 of the Treaty of Versailles (the sanctions), in which the

German leaders were charged with being exclusively responsible for the World War.

Among the French authors who believed that the German confession of war guilt was wrongfully extorted in Article 231 or that certain French and Russian leaders were responsible for launching the war will be found George DeMartial, Gustave Dupin, G. de Toury, A. Pevet, Emile Laloy, René Marchand, Colonel Converset, Alcide Ebray, Lazare, Victor Margueritte, Millon, Mathias Morhardt, A. Fabre-Luce, Ernest Renauld, Ernest Judet, J. Caillaux, Charles Humbard, et al. (See Supplement.)

Among the British authors of like opinion appear E. D. Morel, J. M. Keynes, Francis Neilson, G. P. Gooch, G. Lowes Dickinson, Raymond Beazley, Edith Durham, Irene Cooper Willis, et al.

Among the American authors of like opinion are Professor Sidney B. Fay, Professor Harry Elmer Barnes, Professor Ferdinand Schevill, Charles E. Tansill, historical expert, Library of Congress, E. F. Henderson, Frederick Bausman, W. L. Langer, James W. Thompson, et al.

The Ex-Premier of Italy, Francisco Nitti, has written strongly to like effect in a number of volumes. The revisionist viewpoint is supported by such Italian scholars as Corrado Barbagallo, Augusto Torre and Alberto Lombroso.

In Belgium the new views on war guilt are supported by such scholars as Alcide Ebray and V. de Brabandère; in Sweden by Dr. Aal; in Denmark by Dr. Karl Larsen; in

Holland by Dr. N. Japiske; and in Hungary by Eugene Horwáth, Guillaume de Huszar and John Lutter.

The overwhelming majority of opinion in Russia is that the Czar's Government caused the war, and the succeeding governments gladly gave full publicity to all the secret Russian records from which this fact is demonstrated.

From Serbia we have the "Causes of the World War", by Dr. M. Boghitchevitch, who was the Serbian Minister in Paris and Berlin before the War, and fully confirms the Russian Conspiracy.

In Canada we have John S. Ewart, King's Counsel, who wrote "The Roots and Causes of the Wars 1914-18", after five years of intensive study, giving the evidence in great detail and proving Russian and Entente responsibility.

These historians from Allied countries are among the thousands of intellectuals throughout the world who now know this history. It must be remembered that Marchand's translation of the Black Book "Un Livre Noir", has never been published in English, and was only published in French in 1923, and yet this volume is the official record of secret telegrams proving clearly that the Russian leaders determined on this war, and took the successive persistent steps during a period of twenty-two years—1892-1914—to bring it about.

Under the United States Senate Resolution (1925) to collate the evidence on the origin of the World War, Charles E. Tansill, expert historian, was assigned the task and is now convinced of the Russian and French responsibility. His book has not been published as a Government document for reasons of diplomatic amity.

A list of the more interesting bibliography is attached as an exhibit to this volume. A sweeping acknowledgment is made to these authorities for the evidence in this volume.

III. Why the Truth Is Unknown.

A natural question arises: "How is it that a truth of such gigantic consequence has not been made known to all the world and freely recognized?"

The answer is simple—These most secret archives were not published or known until some years after the war, and when they were disclosed, naturally those who had carried on the pre-war propaganda, and the war-time propaganda in which not only the German Government but the German people were bitterly denounced as the enemies of mankind, were not disposed to confess that they had been parties to an unsound propaganda against the German people. The international press, outside of Germany, had denounced the Germans as guilty of the crime of unloosing the war, and then charged the German troops with every crime in the calendar—cutting off the hands of babies, bayoneting women with child, crucifying soldiers, committing massacres on noncombatants; boiling their own dead to make glycerine for explosives, etc., etc., etc. Every artifice was used to make all the world hate the German name.

These war-time accusations of wholesale atrocities are no

longer believed by informed people. All armies contain some individuals who exhibit atrocity during the terrible excitement of war. The story of cutting off the children's hands was thoroughly investigated, and found untrue. The story of boiling the German dead to get the fat from their bodies was proved to be the confessed invention of a British officer. The press of the world, finding it embarrassing to reverse the views previously believed in, and by which the world was misled, seems to prefer the position that the question of war guilt was settled by the Treaty of Versailles and need not be reopened. They, therefore, have failed as a rule to give publicity to the recently discovered facts or to take the labor and pains to investigate. For this reason, the people of the world have not had access to the truth except through books (such as those written by the authors to whom I have referred), whose circulation is small.

The American press is a giant and has a giant's responsibility. Ultimately, when it knows the truth, it will do its full duty.

Another obstacle to the knowledge of the evidence is Entente official opposition. The Treaty of Versailles (Article 231) had compelled the German leaders to accept complete responsibility for the war. It was not a treaty of agreement. It was a treaty dictated by the victors, and the conquered Germans (over their vehement protests) were compelled to sign the confession of guilt under the threat, after they had disarmed, of being invaded and devastated by war by the Allied armies. The German women and children were suffering the extremities of death by starvation under an Allied embargo as a means of coercing German consent to the dictated treaty. The Germans still strenuously protest they did not will the war. The Treaty of Versailles violated many of the 14 points under which President Woodrow Wilson and the Entente Allies obtained the German consent to the Armistice. For these reasons, the governmental powers of Europe, outside of Germany, were unwilling to have any publicity given to the truth that a few Russian and French leaders had willed this war and forced it on the German leaders, on Europe and on the world. Therefore, the evidence has been largely suppressed by the leaders of the Entente nations.

But the truth disclosed by the evidence cannot be kept permanently concealed, and the scholars of the whole world are now quite well advised with regard to the evidence.

The facts set forth in this book are based upon the evidence of the official records of the belligerent governments, and the particular records listed in Exhibit A will be found to completely justify every important statement made in this work.

There are those who, accepting the facts of the evidence disclosed, still attempt to put the responsibility of the world war upon the German leaders on the theory that the German leaders had no legal right to object to Russia's exercise of her sovereign powers of mobilizing within her own borders; that Russia had a legal right to mobilize within her own borders and that until she actually invaded Germany the German leaders had no right to declare "a state of war existing". But these apologists are compelled to confess that the military menace of Russian mobilization under secret contract to attack Germany on an undefended frontier, with no natural boundaries and no adequate forces, exposed the German military leaders to absolute destruction, if they had failed to mobilize against such a military menace and recognize it for what it was—war.

The evidence shows that the general mobilization of Russia was itself a declaration of war, according to instructions given and understood by the Russian leaders, and, infinitely more important, the evidence now obtained discloses that there WAS a secret contract of 1892 (kept actively alive by annual secret military conference to 1914) between the Russian and French leaders simultaneously to attack Germany "at the first indication" of Austrian mobilization.

In 1892 Gen. de Boisdeffre, representing France, said to the Czar, in construing the Secret Treaty of that date which pledged Russia and France to attack Germany if one of the Powers of the Triple Alliance should mobilize: "Mobilization IS war." Alexander III replied: "That is as I understand it."

The evidence shows that the German leaders made a strenuous effort to prevent the local conflict between Austria and Servia from leading to a general European war, and that the German leaders were not supported either in St. Petersburg, or Paris in this attempt to prevent a European war, but were prevented from localizing the war, or adjusting it by a concert of the powers, by the Russian leaders. *Austria intended a local war* and was *opposed to a general war.*

The war against Serbia into which Austria was deliberately incited by the ruinous intrigues of Serbia at the instigation of Russia *was a trap* into which Austria fell, not knowing it was fomented by Russia to create the pretext of general mobilization and war and to make Austria and Germany appear to the world as the wilful originators of the great conflict.

But the Russian Imperialists are convicted by the secret treaties, military conventions, dispatches, documents and by the confessions out of their own mouths—for example (1914):

Gen. de Boisdeffre—"Mobilization is War." Alexander III agreed that Mobilization is an act of War.

Sazonoff, July 24.—"This is the European War."

Sukhomlinoff, July 25.—"This time we shall march."

Isvolski, August 1.—"This is my war."

Grand Duke Nicholas' wife, Anastasia, quotes code message from her father, King of Montenegro (July 22): "We shall have war before the month is out."

Grand Duke Peter's wife, Melitza (Anastasia's sister), to Paleologue, July 22: "You will get Alsace Lorraine back— our armies will meet in Berlin—Germany will be annihilated," etc., etc., etc.

General Dobrorolski, declared that the War was definitely determined, on July 25th. Pashitch, Serbian Premier, stated

July 31st that the Russian peace negotiations were merely to conceal War. The Russian General Palizyn confirms Pashitch see Supplement, Sec. 25 and 29.

In 1916 Sazonoff admitted that the World War was brought on in 1914 by the determination of France and Russia to humiliate Germany.

Colonel E. M. House wrote to the President of the United States, from Europe May 29, 1914, (House, II, 248):

"Whenever England consents, France and Russia will close in on Germany and Austria."

CHAPTER II

PRE-WAR TENSION IN EUROPE

I. RUSSIA

In the attempt to arrive at a just understanding of the factors making possible the World War, it is necessary to consider the psychology of the various then governing leaders of the nations occupying Europe.

The Russian Government, under the Romanoff family, had gradually acquired powers of absolute monarchy over an area equal to about one-sixth of all the land in the world, and autocratic power over approximately 170,000,000 people speaking many languages and dialects. The policy of the Russian Government was to expand its power and its territory whenever and wherever possible. It was this policy which led to the war with Japan. It was this policy that made the Russian Government desire to exercise hegemony over the Balkans and led to the secret treaties with Serbia, and Bulgaria, setting up the Czar as an arbiter over Balkan disputes, having him pose as the protector of all the people of Slav extraction. The Russian Government deeply desired the control of Constantinople and the Dardanelles as an outlet for the free passage in war of her battleships. Russia desired not only to exercise hegemony over the Balkans, but was secretly and intensively behind the Pan-Slav Movement, which had for its object the disintegration of the Austro-Hungarian Empire and the seizure ultimately of Austrian territory. Russia financed the Pan-Slav movement, especially using Serbia as the instrument, subsidizing the Serbian press and its officers for that purpose.

The Russian imperialists were jealous of the German Empire and coveted German and Austrian territory and negotiated a secret treaty with the French leaders to take a part of it. To carry out these objects, Russia built up the greatest army in Europe, estimated by the Russian press in 1914 as containing 2,230,000 men ready for quick action, and having over 14,000,000 men subject to a call to the colors, according to Dobrorolski, General in charge of mobilization.

In order to carry out the ambitions of the absolute monarchy of Russia, not only were secret agreements made with Roumania, Bulgaria and Serbia, but, still more important, a secret agreement was made with the President of France in 1892, contemplating a simultaneous attack on Germany by Russia and France. In order to make this attack successful, it was essential not only to build up the military and naval powers of Russia and France to a maximum, but it was also necessary to subsidize the Russian and the French press, and persuade public opinion of the honor, patriotism and wisdom of the Russian government in its alleged policies, the real policies never being exposed.

The terrible cruelty and corruption of the Russian military autocracy had built up in Russia a very widespread, deep-set revolutionary spirit, of which the belligerent section appeared through organized nihilism. It was believed by many of the governing officers of Russia that a general war against aliens would excite the patriotism of the Russian people and consolidate them behind the government. Eventually after Russia's collapse in the World War, this revolutionary spirit in Russia proved to be more hostile to the Romanoff autocracy and supporting intelligencia than it was to the alien enemy. It turned on the imperialists with destructive ferocity, tearing down the old standards of government and even the State religion. The Bolshevik regime with Lenine followed.

In the spring of 1914, Russia through France finally had arrived at a gentleman's agreement with the British Government, through Edward Grey. Russia also had a gentleman's agreement with Italy. In 1914 Russia's preparations for war were adequate for the great adventure.

II. BALKAN STATES

The Balkan states, Roumania, Bulgaria and Serbia, and Turkey and Greece, during the several years preceding the World War had engaged in three different wars, all of them inspired by a spirit of militarism and imperialism, seeking to obtain advantages, commercial and political, at the expense of their neighbors. They had all developed the spirit of militarism, and had built up their armies to the extent of their taxing power. The Serbian leaders were determined on the policy of Pan-Slavism and a "Greater Serbia" at the expense of Austria. The Serb press was violent against Austria. At Russia's instigation Serbia plotted war against Austria, for the disintegration of that nation; and some of its military officers took an active part in planning the assassination of the Austrian Grand Duke.

The Balkan Alliance out of which these wars arose was constructed under Russia's auspices.

III. ITALY

Italy, whose government had a defensive alliance with Germany, and Austria, had become ambitious to expand its powers, and had entered upon a substantial colonization policy in Northern Africa. Italy was only bound to support Austria or Germany in the event of a war of wilfull aggression against Germany or Austria, and Italy was not bound if Germany or Austria were held to be the aggressor. Before the World War began, Italy's African interests and her desire for future expansion were utilized by France, Great Britain and Russia to weaken the alliance between Italy, Germany and Austria, and Italy became a dead weight on Germany and Austria. Italy's support could no longer be depended on. After the war began, Italy was given certain other promises by the Entente Allies and fought Austria and Germany.

When the World War came on, it was an important part of the strategy of Russia and France to make Germany and Austria appear as the aggressors, in order that Italy would have the justification of refusing to co-operate with Germany and Austria. This plan worked out successfully through the Pan-Slav movement, the murder of the Archduke of Austria and the violent propaganda carried on in Serbia against Austria. This political intrigue accomplished its intended purpose and led Austria, through the grief of the Emperor's household and the indignation of the Austrian Court, to the conviction that Austria was justified in the use of stern measures to secure guarantees against Servia. The Austrian ultimatum and mobilization followed.

The ultimatum given by Austria to Serbia, the instant military measures of Serbia, Russia, France and Belgium and the war which was declared to exist by Germany on August 1, 1914, enabled the Italian Government to refrain from supporting Austria and Germany on the allegation that Germany and Austria were the aggressors and not the aggrieved—that they had first declared war.

A famous Frenchman, Montesquieu, said a great while ago that:

> "The true author of a war is not he who declares it, but he who makes it necessary."

The European diplomats thoroughly well understand this doctrine, but the mass of mankind did not understand it or its intimate application when the World War was made to come by Russian mobilization and influence.

IV. FRANCE

The French people are largely of Latin extraction, inter-
mingled, however, with the blood of the North. They are
a proud and excitable race, intelligent, artistic, of great
social grace, with a language of the highest degree of mental
refinement. There is no society in the world more charming
than that of the best French circles. Their architecture,
paintings, literature are models of beauty and the admiration
of the world. They have had a very warlike history. They
seem to rejoice in "Glory". Their leaders seem to favor
militarism, though disclaiming it. When the French Revolution was followed by Napoleon, Napoleon conquered nearly
all of continental Europe, and was adored by the French, who
still honor his memory as the greatest of all Frenchmen.
His tomb is a Mecca. In 1870, the French Emperor, Napoleon III, declared war against Germany, and in a few
months the Germans dictated a humiliating peace to the
French at Versailles, imposing a tax of a billion dollars on
the French, and taking over the government of Alsace-Lorraine, which became a terra irredenta and a poisoned thorn
in the side of sensitive France. This all gave birth to the
doctrine of "Revanche" or revenge, which finally bore terrible fruit.

Raymond Poincaré was born in Lorraine, and long before
he had the opportunity of power, and came into the presi-
dency of France (1912), he had set his heart on the restoration of these provinces. In an address at the Uni-

versity of Paris, October, 1920, Poincaré expressed his sentiments in these burning words: "I have not been able to see any other reason for my generation living, except the hope of recovering our lost provinces."

It was this spirit which in 1892 enabled the Russian leaders, in pursuance of their own imperial policies, to make a treaty secretly with the President of France, by which it was agreed that Russia and France should attack Germany simultaneously, in the event of a certain contingency, which the Russian leaders knew they could create, to-wit: "the mobilization" of Austria. They camouflaged this mobilization of Austria under these terms:

"In case the forces of the Triple Alliance, or of one of the powers which are a party to it, should be mobilized (e.g. Austria), France and Russia, *at the first indication* of the event, and *without a previous agreement* being necessary, *shall mobilize all of their forces immediately and simultaneously,* and shall transport them as near to their frontiers as possible. * * * *These forces shall begin complete action with the greatest dispatch,* so that *Germany will have to fight at the same time in the East and in the West."*

After this treaty was entered into by the French President with the Russian leaders, the Russian leaders subsequently borrowed seven billions of dollars from the French people, by selling Russian bonds to them, and using a portion of the proceeds of the bonds to subsidize the French Press, so that it would commend with enthusiasm the value of the investment in Russian securities, and favor a strong Franco-Russian policy in the Balkans. The French leaders required, however, the money to be employed in building up a great Russian army, in the manufacture of light and heavy artillery, in building military strategic railroads, leading up to the German border, etc., and in preparing for the war contemplated by this treaty.

The French, during all these years, from 1870, had been developing great areas in Africa, where they governed between fifty and sixty million African people, recruiting African troops and training them in modern warfare. This provided a means of making available for war a French-controlled population larger than the German population.

The building up of the huge Russian army caused Germany to strengthen its military equipment, and thereupon, when Poincaré became President, the French extended the time of military service for the young men of France from two years to three years, thus increasing this force by 50 per cent. In the meantime, year after year, the French General Staff held military conventions with the Russian General Staff, planning the ways and means by which a war of *offense* could be made against Germany.

France had an understanding with the Italian leaders by 1902 and both France and Russia began to compose all differences with Great Britain in 1904-1907.

France, through its Ambassador at London, negotiated in 1912 a secret agreement with Edward Grey, which purported not to be an agreement, but merely an exchange of letters, in which it was recited that in the event an occasion of war should arise in which the co-operation of the French and British Government might be deemed desirable, that the question of common action should be immediately discussed and if it "involved action the plans of the general staffs would at once be taken into consideration and the governments would then decide what effect should be given to them."

This hypothetical alliance was gradually strengthened. Military and naval plans were worked out between the French and British officers. It was agreed that France could withdraw its entire fleet from the West coast of France to the Mediterranean, that the British fleet would protect the French coast, and that Great Britain would put 160,000 men on the left wing of the French army, all of which was duly carried out when the war took place the first of August, 1914.

When Raymond Poincaré became President (with treaty-making powers) he immediately and repeatedly assured the Russian statesmen that they could rely with confidence upon the diplomatic support of Russian policy in the Balkans, and upon the French support in case of a general war flowing therefrom. The week before Russian mobilization Poincaré was in St. Petersburg strengthening the Russian will to war. (See Paléologue, Ewart, Barnes, Morhardt.) When the general war grew more intensely threatening he refused to try to exercise any moderating influence with Russia. He alone could have prevented war. He did not because he willed war.

V. Great Britain

The British interest was quite different. The tremendous strides made by the Germans in industrial production, ship-building, and commerce, and finally the ambition of the Kaiser to build up a big navy disturbed many British leaders. They began to view Germany as a somewhat dangerous rival and looked with increasing hostility upon the proposed German naval expansion. The intensive military training of the German youth, the Prussian military system, probably the most efficient in the world, and the Hohenzollern monarchy were regarded with aversion and increasing apprehension. According to the controlling British view, if the Prussian military machine should conquer France, it would dominate Europe and this consideration, with the others mentioned, probably led Edward Grey to believe the agreement with Cambon justified.

When the Czar mobilized under Poincaré's encouragement and war ensued involving Germany and France, the British statesmen were moved by what they believed to be best for the British Government. The invasion of Belgium was a pretext and not the cause for the declaration of war by Great Britain. The newly published English documents bear out the above conclusions.

VI. Germany

In 1914 Germany had no reason for war, no terra irredenta, no revenge and knew that a general European war might easily destroy its merchant marine, its foreign commerce, both of which were rapidly expanding, and cause the loss of its colonies.

Between 1870 and 1914, under the German Empire, the productive power of the German people had been tremendously increased by systematic, technical education of the German youth in all the industries, arts and sciences. The German schools and universities had attained the distinction of being the finest in the world. At Dusseldorf, the German Government promoted the establishment of a manufacturing system where every kind of manufacturing enterprise in Germany was represented, and the custom was established to permit students of the higher grades from all parts of Germany to visit Dusseldorf and examine these plants in action, so that they might select the life-work for which their tastes inclined them.

Co-operative credit, co-operative buying and selling, municipal management of public utilities and other democratic processes were stimulated, but the central power was very firmly held under the Hohenzollern regime. The German people were happy and prosperous and intensely patriotic.

Germany like other nations had its jingoes and super-patriots who rejoiced in war talk, like von Bernhardi. William II posed as a War Lord at times and assiduously cultivated his army and navy in the hope of protecting Germany from attack by a show of power.

The German Emperor, however, and his advisers during forty years made no war on others. William II claimed and

believed that he was a powerful force for the preservation
of the peace of Europe. The people of Germany were great
home-lovers, and had large families. They were social, fond
of music, and developed music unsurpassed in the world.
The capital of Germany, Berlin, in the uniform excellence
of its architecture, of its streets, of its public conveniences
and parks, and the economy of living was unsurpassed. The
people were not only industrious, but they were thrifty, and
Germany very rapidly grew in wealth, in commercial and
financial power. The Germans desired security and peace,
but believing that they were surrounded by dangerous enemies, the spirit of nationalism, of patriotism and military
training was stimulated to the highest degree, and they, like
the other people of Europe, were ready to die for the defense
of their country.

It was entirely against the interests of Germany to engage
in war. The Germany of Schiller and Goethe, of Wagner
and Beethoven hated war. The German leaders were against
war and feared it.

Just as the enormous military preparations of Russia excited the fears of the German leaders, so the German preparations excited the fears and anger of the French leaders
and strengthened those who were plotting for war.

The Prussian military machine, with its general staff, was
probably the most efficient war machine ever constructed.
Its officers lived an intensive, military, self-sacrificing existence. They were given extraordinary honors by the civil-
ian population on all occasions. They were the men who

had pledged their lives for the peace and security of the country. They held their profession in supreme honor. The German army was full of inherited tradition. German valor and efficiency were unsurpassed. The Germans knew they were surrounded by enemies, much more numerous than they, and of equal intelligence, and that they could only make up for their disadvantage by courage, speed and skill. They had annual maneuvers, the officers were constantly at work studying the art of war, and the scientific men of Germany were co-operating in metals and in chemicals to make improved engines of war.

The reputation of the Prussian military machine went abroad, and neighboring nations regarded it with fear. Its great efficiency was conceded, so that when the time came for Russia to begin the attack on Germany, it was of great importance, in the Russian view, that the Russian mobilization should have the advantage over the German mobilization of at least a week to ten days. The military conventions between the French and Russian Staffs assert that it probably would be the 15th day before Russian armies could get into full action, whereas either Germany or France could probably get into action within a week or ten days. For this reason, it was absolutely essential, from a Russian military standpoint, that the Russians *should on July 24, 1914, camouflage their military measures,* and prevent the Germans from knowing their serious military plans. The Germans, from reliable reports, did know what it was; and the German military attaché at St. Petersburg flatly rejected the representations of the Russian chief of staff to his face when an attempt was made to make it appear that there had been no mobilization whatever.

VII. BELGIUM

The lands of Belgium between the German and French territory are level, with no natural defenses. They comprise a densely settled rich section occupied by industrious, productive and highly cultivated people closely bound by many ties to France. The people generally speak French and use the franc for currency.

Because of its geographical location, this region had been frequently a battleground in the past. Belgian leaders had made every effort to obtain a position of guaranteed neutrality, and an agreement of other nations that this neutrality should be respected, but the military strategists of Europe recognizing that "necessity knows no law", universally regarded it as a certainty that in the event of war between Germany and France, Belgium would be employed as a necessary corridor for the entry into France of German troops, because the French border, otherwise protected by mountains and hills, had been so thoroughly fortified that a passway was impossible. The demonstration of this was shown at Verdun, where the Germans lost 500,000 men in an attempt to break through, and never were able to pass. The interest of the Belgian people required their government to co-operate with France and Great Britain as against Germany, and there was a gentleman's agreement as to this co-operation, although the Belgian authorities greatly desired to strictly preserve their legal, technical position of defending their neutrality against any invasion. The only invasion which they had occasion to anticipate and the only invasion against which they prepared was the invasion of German troops. The European strategists knew that in the event of a war involving France and Germany the German general staff would be compelled to attack France through Belgium.

Belgium relied upon French and British support against Germany, and did not seek or rely upon Germany support against a French invasion. As a matter of military strategy, the French did not need access to Germany through Belgium. At the outbreak of the war Belgian authorities were notified not to regard French entry on Belgian territory as an offense.

The Duchy of Luxemburg, like Belgium, was necessary also as a passway to or from France, but unlike Belgium, Luxemburg had no powers of defense, and could do nothing more than make a gesture against the passage of alien troops. Belgium had a strong army. The forts next to the German border were well designed, for defense, and were able in August, 1914, for several weeks to stay the advance of the German troops. Belgium with magnificent bravery refused to allow Germany to violate its neutrality and suffered terribly in consequence. It was a victim of fate as a result of the Russian intrigue.

VIII. Switzerland

Switzerland, which is a republic consisting of German, French and Italian people, speaking all three languages, was and is a modern republic of highly cultivated, brave people. Their country was easily defensible because of the gigantic mountain ranges, thoroughly fortified, and with an efficient militia of 600,000 men. None of the belligerents could afford, as a matter of military strategy, to violate the neutrality of Switzerland, and none of them attempted it.

IX. The High Seas

The enormous war fleet of Great Britain, consisting of over 400 vessels, absolutely commanded the Atlantic Ocean, the North Sea and the entrance to the Baltic. The entire German merchant marine was paralyzed by the war. The French fleet withdrawn from the Atlantic controlled the Mediterranean Sea against Germany.

X. Imperialism

All the nations of Europe had contributed to the building up of the spirit of militarism, in which they had engendered fear of each other and mutual animosities, because of threats, real or implied, in their imperialistic and acquisitive policies, and all of the great nations, as also the Balkans contributed in this sense to the spirit of war which made it possible by intrigue to bring about the catastrophe of 1914.

None of the European belligerent governments can be entirely absolved from responsibility for creating conditions which made war possible.

It was the common doctrine of Europe that the only way to prevent invasion and war on one's country was to be thoroughly prepared "for defense". This was the doctrine of the civilians as well as the military caste, but the military caste went further and held that the best way in which to wage defensive war was by waging an *offensive* war. The military plan was to strike first. This doctrine is clearly set up in concrete terms in the minutes of the annual military conferences between the Russian and the French General Staffs.

All the great nations of Europe had cultivated the policy of colonial expansion, taking over territory throughout the world, occupied by weaker and defenseless people, and had excited rivalries between each other, which in Africa had brought about serious tension between France and its allies and Germany.

All these conditions contributed to the success of the intrigues which led to the World War. In pursuance of these policies all the nations of Europe were well armed. There was a rivalry in armament and in preparations for war. The people were led to support these policies by propaganda in the public press advocating preparedness for defense. It proved to be preparedness for offense.

France, Germany, Austria, Russia and Serbia had their jingoes, who praised war and stirred up fear and hate, but the real power was in a few hands and it was the cold-blooded will to war of Isvolski, Sazonoff, Grand Duke Nicholas, and others in Russia, and of Poincaré, Delcassé, Viviani, Millerand, et al. in France that launched it.

The German Kaiser was convinced that a war of the Entente allies against Germany meant the defeat of Germany and his own political destruction and on July 30, 1914, made a written record of this conviction. He did his utmost to prevent it.

CHAPTER III

WAR PLANS AND WAR BOOTY

I. How the World War Was Engineered By a Very Few Men

The evidence of how the World War took place is now quite complete. It was engineered by the Russian officials in control of Russian foreign affairs, led by Isvolski, former Minister of Foreign Affairs of the Russian Empire, and in the years preceding the war Russian Ambassador to France.

A microscopic study has been made of Isvolski. His letters and dispatches have been analyzed and indexed and printed in great detail by Frederich Stieve, René Marchand and others. His personal relation to the plotting of the war appears in the book "Isvolski and the World War", by Stieve. In May, 1906, Isvolski was placed at the head of the Foreign Office of the Russian Empire. Shortly before this, in March, 1906, he went to Paris, where he met three other Russian diplomats—Count Benckendorff, Russian Ambassador to London; Nelidov, Russian Ambassador to Paris, and Muravieff, Russian Ambassador in Rome. There was an exchange of views between the four men, at which it was agreed to develop the Triple Entente between Russia, France and

Great Britain. The new Foreign Minister informed the Czar of the results when he took over the seals of office. Isvolski himself describes it as the program—

"Of which the further development led to the system of the Triple Entente,"

in which it was determined by the four Ambassadors to reinforce the alliance of France by agreements with Great Britain and Japan.

Immediately after he took office, he began to work towards a rapprochement with Great Britain and her ally Japan. On July 30, 1907, a convention was concluded between Russia and Japan, clearing up all existing differences. On August 31, 1907, a convention was concluded at St. Petersburg between Great Britain and Russia, covering all points at issue between the two powers in regard to Afghanistan, Tibet and Persia.

Isvolski's aims harmonized with the London policies of King Edward VII of encircling Germany. The Entente of Great Britain was cemented by the meeting of the British King and the Czar, at Reval in June, 1908.

It was in pursuance of this policy of building up the Triple Entente against the so-called Triple Alliance that the treaty concluded in 1905 at Bjorkoe between the German Emperor and Czar Nicholas II, proposing friendly relations between Germany, Russia and France, was refused ratification.

The adverse influence of the French leaders and of the Triple Entente prevented various other efforts made by the

Germans to establish a rapprochement severally with Great Britain, with France and with Russia. The sinister and dangerous objects which Isvolski and the Russian and French leaders had in view are completely disclosed by the dispatches published in "Entente Diplomacy and the World War", by de Siebert, in "Un Livre Noir", by René Marchand, and in the Isvolski Papers, by Frederick Stieve. The de Siebert publication gives 856 secret dispatches between the Russian Foreign Office and Benckendorff, the Russian Ambassador at London. "Un Livre Noir" gives about a like number of secret dispatches, passing between the Russian Foreign Office and the Russian Ambassador, Isvolski, in Paris.

These dispatches day by day, of the most intimate secret character, demonstrate clearly and positively the Russian policy. That policy was that the Russians must have control of the Dardanelles, as a means of giving free access to the world markets for Russian products, and second, the extension of Russian influence in the Balkans and to the West against Germany and Austria, an object which could only be attained by a general European war in which Russia, France, Great Britain, with the Balkan allies, should overthrow Germany. The Russian Imperialists had clearly in view the considerations which would be offered to various allies in order to induce their co-operation in a general war against Germany.

First, was the ambition of the few French leaders who controlled the Foreign Policy of France. They wished to obtain the restoration of Alsace and Lorraine, the great iron mines of Lorraine, the coal properties of the Saar Valley, revenge on Germany for the indignity and humiliation inflicted by the Franco-Prussian War of 1871 and to break down the growing power of Germany. The French Government got what it was after, but the expense was larger than had been anticipated by Poincaré.

The co-operation of Serbia was secured by promising and giving Serbia Russian support in the Pan-Slav movement for a "Greater Serbia", in which it was proposed that the Pan-Slav population of Austria and adjacent country and the territory occupied by them should be made a part of "Greater Serbia". The Serbian Government, as Jugo-Slavia, got what the leaders sought.

Roumania was to be satisfied by obtaining Transylvania, which she got and now holds. Bulgaria was to be made a secret ally by supporting certain of her pretensions. Bulgaria was also committed to Germany and thus got nothing. Great Britain was to be moved to co-operate with France in the event of a war between France and Germany, on the ground that Germany had become a rival to be reckoned with commercially; that Germany was building up a navy that threatened British supremacy at sea; that German military autocracy, if it were allowed to conquer France, would control Western Europe, and would become a menace to British interests.

This Russian intrigue was politically possible between Isvolski and his associates and the French leaders because, under the Constitution of 1875, the President of France had the right (and still has the right) to make a secret treaty on his sole authority, binding France without the advice or consent of the French Senate or the French Parliament.

Joseph Barthélemy, French professor of political science, in "Democracy and Foreign Policy," 1917, makes the following statement of the principles of the French constitution of 1875:[1]

"The constitution of 1875 was the result of a transaction brought about, among other things, by the force of co-operation between *a monarchist majority* unable to establish a monarchy and a republican minority.

"First, in principle, the President of the Republic alone represents the nation in foreign affairs; it is to him are accredited the ambassadors of foreign powers; it is in his name in which the ambassadors of France speak; he conducts the negotiations; it is by his signature that he binds the country in international treaties of which he is the juridical author."

"The principle expressly set forth by Article 8 of the law of the 16th of July, 1875, is that the President of the Republic negotiates and ratifies treaties upon his sole authority."[2]

"Almost all of the great international acts which have marked the turning point of our foreign policies during the half-century, almost all those which have exercised a decisive influence on the destinies of France, are the work of the Government alone and have been ratified by the President of the Republic upon his sole authority. It is in effect that Article 8 of the law of the 16th of July 1875, does not submit to parliamentary approval the most important perhaps of all the treaties, the great political treaties and the treaties of alliance."[3]

[1] Op. cit. p. 102.
[2] Op. cit. p. 105.
[3] Op. cit. p. 109.

It was under this authority that the *profoundly secret* treaty between Russia and France of 1892 contemplating military operations against Germany was executed and withheld from the knowledge of the French Parliament and from the French people. It was under this authority that the *secret* treaties of 1916-17 to divide German and Austrian territory between France and Russia were entered into.

Great Britain's foreign affairs are directed in like fashion by the British Foreign Office, No. 10 Downing Street, without necessarily being directed by or even disclosed to the British Parliament.

Sir Edward Grey, in his agreements with the Governments of France and Russia, contemplating military and naval co-operation between Russia, France and Great Britain along the lines worked out by the military and naval staffs of the three countries, was able to do so in *absolute secrecy*. He did not submit these records to Parliament until after the war had been entered into by Great Britain. Six times the British Parliament was advised that there were no commitments made.[1]

It is of supreme international importance that the world should understand the structure of these foreign offices and what they did in bringing about the World War.[2]

The imperial structure of the French and British governments still so exist.

[1] "How Diplomats Make War", Neilson; "Entente Diplomacy and the World"; "Un Livre Noir", etc.
[2] Congressional Record, 355-356.

II. The Franco-Russian Treaty of 1892-4

It was in pursuance of this French law that the following secret treaty was entered into in 1892 between the Minister of Foreign Affairs of Russia and the President of the French Republic and concluded in 1894.

The French issued after the war, when they first disclosed the terms of this agreement, a special Yellow Book upon this subject. The essential terms of it can be found in the pamphlet of March, 1919, No. 136, of the American Association for International Conciliation. The body of the engagement is as follows:

"France and Russia, animated by a common desire to preserve the peace, and having no other end in mind than to ward off the necessities of a defensive war, provoked by an attack of the forces of the Triple Alliance against either of them, have agreed upon the following provision": (This self-serving declaration of innocence might be useful if the secret treaty should be exposed.)

"*1. If France is attacked by Germany, or by Italy, supported by Germany, Russia shall employ all its available forces to fight Germany.*"

"*2. In case the forces of the Triple Alliance, or of one of the powers which are a party to it,*" (e.g. Austria) "*should be mobilized, France and Russia, at the first indication of the event, and without a previous agreement being necessary, shall mobilize all their forces immediately and simultaneously, and shall transport them as near to their frontiers as possible.*"

"*3. The available forces which must be employed against Germany shall be: For France, 1,300,000 men; for Russia, from 700,000 to 800,000 men.*" (France in 1913 pledged 200,000 more and in 1914 Russia had 2,230,000 men ready.)

"*These forces shall begin complete action with the greatest dispatch,*"

*so that Germany will have to fight at the same time in the east and in
the west."*

*"4. The staffs of the armies of the two countries shall constantly
plan in concert in order to prepare for and facilitate the execution of
the measures set forth above."*

*"They shall communicate to each other, in time of peace, all the in-
formation regarding the armies of the Triple Alliance which is in, or
shall come into, their possession."*

*"The ways and means of corresponding in time of war shall be
studied and arranged in advance."*

"5. France and Russia shall not conclude a separate peace."

*"6. The present convention shall have the same duration as the
Triple Alliance."* (Later extended beyond such duration.)

*"7. All the clauses enumerated above shall be kept absolutely
secret."* [1] ... ...

In defending the instant attack on Germany if Germany or
Austria should mobilize as contemplated by this Secret
Treaty General de Boisdeffre for France said: "Mobilization
is War." Alexander III replied: "I so regard it."

III. THE FRANCO-RUSSIAN MILITARY CONFERENCES

In pursuance of this treaty, the Russian and French General Staffs had many conferences to determine the plans and
methods for making the assault on Germany.

The minutes of three of these meetings of 1911, 1912 and
1913 were inserted in the Congressional Record of December
18, 1923, on pages 358 to 362, inclusive.

In the preamble to each of these meetings appears the following remarkable declaration of principle:

[1] Congressional Record, 357.

"The two chiefs of staff declare, by common accord, that the words 'defensive war' must not be interpreted in the sense of a war which would be conducted defensively. They affirm, on the contrary, the absolute necessity for the Russian and French armies to adopt a vigorous offensive, and as far as possible a simultaneous one, in conformity with the text of Article 3 of the convention, whose terms provide that 'the forces of the two contracting powers shall come into full action with all speed.'"

The "defensive" war proposed was strictly for diplomatic purposes it will be observed. The French words of this secret treaty were: "Les forces des deux puissances contractantes s'engagent a fond et en toute diligence." [1]

Article 1 declares:

"The two chiefs of staff, confirming the viewpoint of preceding conferences, are entirely in accord on the point that the defeat of the German armies remains, whatever the circumstances may be, the first object of the allied armies." [2]

In Article 3 the French Chief of Staff submitted the following consideration:

"From what is known of the German mobilization and concentration, one may conclude that the first great encounters will probably take place in Lorraine, Luxemburg and Belgium from the fifteenth to the eighteenth day," (so vanishes the legend of the shocked surprise with which the allied Governments learned of the German invasion of Belgium).

"At that moment the strength of the French Army will be greater than the 1,300,000 men provided for by Article 3 of the convention." [3]

[1] Congressional Record, 358.
[2] Congressional Record, 358.
[3] Congressional Record, 358.

The minutes set forth the following:

"This object, which was the very basis of the military convention of 1892, can only be attained by the offensive.

"The effect of this offensive will be more certain insomuch as it will take place sooner, will be carried out with greater strength, and will take a more dangerous direction for the enemy.

"In these circumstances, and it being admitted by common accord by the conferring parties that the Germans will direct the principal mass of their forces against France (so this was no surprise), *the French chief of staff expresses the desire that the disposition (of the Russian armies) should, as far as possible, allow of taking the offensive with the first echelon* (body of troops) *as from the eighteenth day. Perhaps even this delay might be reduced, thanks to the recent improvements introduced into the Russian mobilization and concentration.*

"General Dubail closes his exposition by remarking that he is not unaware of the various motives which have compelled Russia to revise the disposition of her troops upon her territory in time of peace. He renders a sincere homage to the efforts made during the last three years by Russia to reinforce her military power, and he is happy to note the improvement produced, as a whole, and the friendly and allied army by the latest modifications introduced into the mobilization." [1]

General Gilinsky, on behalf of Russia, declares, among other things, that Russia is expanding her forces preparatory to action, and says:

"In these circumstances Russia does not appear to be in a condition to sustain, for two years at least (that is to say, not before 1913. By the spring of 1914, Russia's military chiefs publicly announced their readiness through the organ of the Russian war minister), *a war against Germany with a certainty of success."* [2]

It is therefore clearly apparent that the pretense of the

[1] Congressional Record, 358.
[2] Congressional Record, 359.

French and Russian leaders that they were taken by surprise by Germany is not true; that they well understood that Germany, in a case of war, would have to come through Belgium and Luxemburg; and the pretense that Russia and France were not prepared was a falsehood, *is shown by the secret French and Russian records,* as set forth in these conferences.

The official record evidence of the plan to attack Germany is *Russian* and *French* evidence.

These minutes further declare, Article 4:

"(3) The minutes of the conferences will be submitted to the approval of the government of each country, and a visé of the minister of war and of the prime minister will be attached thereto, so that the chiefs of staffs of the allied armies may refer to this document in the realization of desirable improvements."

So these warlike plans to attack Germany had the approval of the Prime Minister of France and of Russia.[1]

They agreed also not to make peace separately in Article 5, as follows:

"The conferring parties are agreed that Article 5 compels the contracting parties not only not to make peace, but also not to cease operations in order to conclude an armistice, individually." [2]

The military conferences of 1912 and 1913 confirm the previous understandings, and in the conference of August, 1913, appears the following language:

"General Joffre declares that France will engage on its northeast frontier almost all of her forces, the number of which will exceed that

[1] Congressional Record, 359.
[2] Congressional Record, 359.

*provided for in the text of the convention by more than 200,000 men
(that is exceeding 1,500,000 men); that the concentration of the fighting elements on this frontier will be completed, for the most part, on
the tenth day of mobilization and that the offensive operations of this
group of forces will commence from the morning of the eleventh
day."* [1]

Poincaré, President of France, declared to the French
Parliament August 4, 1914, that the French armies were
ready for action. Mobilization must have started eleven
days before or July 24.[2]

These military conferences provided for the double track-
ing of the roads leading to the German frontiers as a means
of quickly mobilizing the Russian troops against Germany.

It is clear that General Joffre pledged 1,500,000 men for
quick action and that their mobilization began July 24, for
they were ready August 4. A large number of these troops
were from the African colonies of France—Moroccans,
Arabs, negroes. Europeans were killing Europeans with
trained Africans. All the records must be interpreted in the
light of this profoundly secret treaty of the Russian and
French leaders to make offensive war on the German people,
who were kept in ignorance of the conspiracy. The very
existence of this secret treaty was denied, and Article 7 of
the agreement itself provided:

*"All the clauses enumerated above shall be kept absolutely
secret."*

These military conventions demonstrated certain truths

[1] Congressional Record, 361.
[2] French Yellow Book, 158. Congressional Record, 373.

now of the first consequence. First, that the pretended un-
preparedness of Russia and of France in July, 1914, was a
colossal willful falseful, intended to deceive the world, support the theory of the innocence of the guilty Russian and
French leaders, and further the theory of the willful guilt
of the German leaders.

Russia, as these military conventions show, was to have
the required light and heavy artillery ready for war by 1914.
The public press of St. Petersburg announced that the available Russian forces were ready, and that they had over
2,000,000 men ready for quick action.

The military conventions were not confined to the heads
of the general staffs of Russia and France, but by their
own terms were to be submitted *"to the approval of the government of each country and a visé of the Minister of War
and of the Prime Minister will be attached thereto."*

The conventions provided for the most complete inter-
communication by messengers, by cable, by radio. The understandings between the Russian and French leaders with
regard to division of German and Austrian territory and
property were not left in doubt, and these agreements will
be found set forth on page 362 of the Congressional Record
of December 18, 1923.

Above all as "Mobilization" was declared to be War by the
Russian and French leaders who made the secret treaty it
follows as a logical necessity that the mobilization of Russia
with French approval July 30th, 1914, and the refusal to stop

it was by the Russian and French understanding an act of war against Germany which began the World War.

The Russians and French thus began the World War. Germany acknowledged its existence and declared it, 7:10 P.M., August 1st, 1914, eight days after it began and two days after it was declared by the decree of Mobilization published throughout Russia.

IV. DIVIDING THE BOOTY OF WAR

Sazonoff on the 24th of February, 1916, wired the Russian Ambassador at Paris, Isvolski, as follows:

"The political agreements concluded between the Allies during the war must remain intact, and are not subject to revision. They include the argreement with France and England on Constantinople, the Straits, Syria and Asia Minor, and also the London treaty with Italy. All suggestions for the future delimitation of central Europe are at present premature, but in general one must bear in mind that we are prepared to allow France and England complete freedom in drawing up the western frontiers of Germany, in the expectation that the Allies on their part would allow us equal freedom in drawing up our frontiers with Germany and Austria."

This meant the Russian statesmen would control Constantinople and the Straits, and take what they pleased of eastern Germany and Austria, while France would take what it pleased of western Germany.

The London treaty with Italy referred to promised Italy various territories belonging to other governments, but which the Italian leaders coveted. This same telegram says:

"Roumania has already been offered all the political advantages which could induce her to take up arms, and therefore it would be perfectly futile to search for new baits in this respect."

The term "bait" is more expressive than polite. It is not the usual language of diplomacy, but served the purpose of conveying the idea of how Sazonoff regarded the great country of Transylvania as *"bait"* which he had thrown to the Roumanian Government, as he might throw the haunch of a stag to a faithful retainer. It probably was useful in assuring the co-operation of some of the Roumanian leaders, although Roumania had powerful ties of blood with Russia and with Great Britain, through the able and beautiful Queen of Roumania, daughter of the Duke of Edinburgh, who was an influence of great power in the decisions of Roumania.

On February 1, 1917, the Russian Foreign Minister addressed the following note to the French Ambassador at Petrograd:

"In your note of today's date your Excellency was good enough to inform the Imperial Government that the Government of the Republic was contemplating the inclusion in the terms of peace to be offered to Germany the following demands and guaranties of a territorial nature:

"1. Alsace-Lorraine to be restored to France.

"2. The frontiers are to be extended at least up to the limits of the former principality of Lorraine and are to be drawn up at the discretion of the French Government so as to provide for the strategic needs and for the inclusion in French territory of the entire iron district of Lorraine and of the entire coal district of the Saar Valley.

"*3. The rest of the territories situated on the left bank of the Rhine, which now form part of the German Empire, are to be entirely separated from Germany and freed from all political and economic dependence upon her.*

"*4. The territories of the left bank of the Rhine outside French territory are to be constituted an autonomous and neutral State, and are to be occupied by French troops until such time as the enemy States have completely satisfied all the conditions and guaranties indicated in the treaty of peace.*

"*Your Excellency stated that the Government of the Republic would be happy to be able to rely upon the support of the Imperial Government for the carrying out of its plans. By order of His Imperial Majesty, my most august master, I have the honor, in the name of the Russian Government, to inform your Excellency by the present note that the Government of the Republic may rely upon the support of the Imperial Government for the carrying out of its plans as set out above.*"

Thus was recorded the promise to the French leaders of what they wanted—Alsace-Lorraine, the coal district of the Saar Valley, the separation of the German country on the west bank of the Rhine from the German Empire as a neutral state, to be occupied by French troops.

On February 26, 1917, Isvolski, the Russian Ambassador, sent the following telegram to M. Pekrovsky:

"*See my reply to telegram No. 167, No. 2. The Government of the French Republic, anxious to confirm the importance of the treaties concluded with the Russian Government in 1915, for the settlement on the termination of the war of the question of Constantinople and the Straits in accordance with Russia's aspirations, anxious, on the other hand, to secure for its ally in military and industrial respects all the guaranties desirable for the safety and the economic development*

of the Empire, recognize Russia's complete liberty in establishing her
western frontiers."

Here a pledge of the French Government to the Russian
Government is recorded, revealing the promised support to
the Russian aspirations as to Constantinople and the Straits,
and:

> *"recognizing Russia's complete liberty in establishing her*
> *western frontier."*

This term "liberty in establishing her western frontier"
is a diplomatic way of expressing the idea of taking territory away from other governments, (Germany and Austria),
by drawing certain lines on the map, and thereafter exercising military and civil jurisdiction over the people included
within the boundaries thus fixed. The usual diplomatic term
employed in the time of Frederick the Great was *"Corriger
la figure"*, meaning to "correct the figure", that is, make the
lines look better on the map.

On February 27, 1917, following the French pledge to
recognize Russia's complete liberty in establishing her
western frontier at the expense of Germany and Austria,
the Russian revolution took place, and three days later the
Czar abdicated. As a consequence, the Imperial Government of the Czar never had an opportunity to "correct the
figure" of Russia on the west, nor to exercise "complete
liberty in establishing her western frontiers," but, on the
contrary, the people of Poland demanded the right of self-
determination and an independent government.

The Russian Soviet Government, being regarded as a menace to the governments of Western Europe, was given no recognition when the time came for establishing new frontiers, but a series of republics was established on what had previously been western Russia in Latvia, Esthonia, Lithuania, Poland; Northern Silesia was attached to Poland with Danzig and part of East Prussia; Czecho-Slovakia was set up, Transylvania was attached to Roumania, and Roumania was expanded on the east by allowing her to take over Bessarabia. Greater Serbia became Jugo-Slavia, at the expense of Austrian territory. Austria became a very small State.

The Entente deprived the Germans of large portions of their Eastern territory as well as other sections on the West and South.

Mr. Balfour on December 19, 1917, denied on behalf of Great Britain any knowledge of the Russian and French plan to cut off western Germany into a new State on the west bank of the Rhine, so it seems that the Russian and French conspirators did not disclose their plan for division of the loot to their most intimate allies.

In 1905 William II aggressively made the Bjorkoe Treaty with the weak Nicholas, pledging German and Russian friendship and inviting France to join. France refused and the treaty was cancelled through Russian and French influence. Nicholas II knew of the treaty with France of 1892 when he signed the Bjorkoe Treaty.

The Triple Entente and Its War Plans

It was in 1906 that the four Russian Ambassadors got together in Paris, determined on the plan of promoting the Triple Entente and that Russia promptly made a settlement of outstanding differences with Japan and Great Britain, and France had already composed its differences with the British Foreign Office. In 1906 Sir Edward Grey, on behalf of the British Government, entered into an agreement with France, which on November 22, 1912, he reduced to writing:

(Letter of Sir Edward Grey to French Ambassador Cambon, November 22, 1912.)

MY DEAR AMBASSADOR: From time to time in recent years the French and British military and naval experts have consulted together. It has always been understood that such consultation does not restrict the freedom of either government to decide at any future time whether or not to assist the other by armed force. We have agreed that consultation between experts is not and ought not be regarded as an engagement that commits either government to action in a contingency that has not yet arisen and may never arise. The disposition, for instance, of the French and British fleets, respectively, at the present moment is not based upon an engagement to co-operate in war.

You have, however, pointed out that if either government have grave reason to expect an unprovoked attack by a third power, it might become essential to know whether it could in that event depend upon the armed assistance of the other.

I agree that if either government had grave reason to expect an unprovoked attack by a third power, or something that threatened the general peace, it should immediately discuss with the other whether both governments should act together to prevent aggression and to preserve peace, and, if so, what measures they would be prepared to take in common.

If these measures involved action, the plans of the general staffs would at once be taken into consideration, and the governments would then decide what effect should be given to them.[1]

The French Ambassador, Cambon, immediately replied in the following letter:

FRENCH EMBASSY,
London, November 23, 1912.

DEAR SIR EDWARD: You remind me in your letter of yesterday, November 22, that during the last few years the military and naval authorities of France and Great Britain had consulted with each other from time to time; that it had always been understood that these consultations should not restrict the liberty of either government to decide in the future whether they should lend each other the support of their armed forces; that on either side these consultations between experts were not and should not be considered as engagements binding our governments to take action in certain eventualities; that, however, I had remarked to you that if one or other of the two governments had grave reasons to fear an unprovoked attack on the part of a third power it would become essential to know whether it could count on the armed support of the other.

Your letter answers that point; and I am authorized to state that in the event of one of our two governments having grave reasons to fear either an attack from a third power or some event threatening the general peace, that government would immediately examine with the other the question whether both governments should act together in order to prevent aggression or preserve peace. If so, the two governments would deliberate as to the measures which they would be prepared to take in common. If those measures involved action, the two governments would take into immediate consideration the plans

[1] *The last vital paragraph was not read to Parliament by Grey,* although afterwards published in the White Book. (How Diplomats Make War 303.)

of their general staffs and would then decide as to the effect to be given to those plans.

Yours, etc.,

PAUL CAMBON.

(How Diplomats Make War, 279.)

VI. MILITARY ARRANGEMENTS AND MOBILIZATION

In 1914 Sir Edward Grey delivered copies of these letters exchanged between him and the French Ambassador to the Russian Ambassador as a basis for an entente between Great Britain and Russia,[1] under which a plan of naval co-operation between Great Britain, Russia and France was worked out.

When the German rulers ordered a German mobilization, 5 P.M., Saturday afternoon, August 1, their action was followed the next morning, Sunday, August 2, 1914,[2] by the marching of regiments through London equipped for war.

French troops invaded German soil Sunday, August 2, 1914.[3]

On Saturday, the 1st day of August, the German border was crossed in four places by Russian patrols.[4]

Germany declared a state of war existing with Russia, because of Russian acts, on August 1, 1914, 7:10 P.M.;[5] with France, August 3, 1914; Belgium, August 4, 1914.

France declared war against Germany on August 3, 1914;

[1] See ch. 12, Entente Diplomacy and the World, p. 709.

[2] How Diplomats Make War, Neilson, p. 295.

[3] Reflections on the World War, p. 145.

[4] Preparation and Conduct of the World War. Von Kuhl, pp. 79-80.

[5] Scott, Documents on World War, p. 1377.

Great Britain against Germany, August 4, 1914; Russia against Germany, August 7, 1914. The evidence appears to show that it was the Russian policy to invade Germany without a declaration of war and to make its mobilization [1] complete under the camouflage of peaceful negotiations.

In the Russian Czar's orders for mobilization, 30th of September, 1912, Chancellor Von Bethmann-Hollweg quotes the following language:

"It is the Emperor's order that the notification of the mobilization should be equivalent to the notification of a state of war with Germany."

In other words, the Russian mobilization order was to be regarded as a secret declaration of war.

The Russian troops invaded Germany before Russia declared war. Hollweg further states that the Russian instruction for the troops on the German front was:

"As soon as concentration is completed we shall proceed to advance against the armed forces of Germany with the object of carrying the war on to their own territory." [2]

This was strictly in line with the Franco-Russian Treaty of 1892 and the military conferences of 1911, 1912 and 1913.

It will be observed that under the Franco-Russian secret treaty of 1892, Section I, it was provided that in case of war Russia should employ all its available forces to fight Germany and that the military and naval staffs, in the military conference above quoted, expressly contemplated that

[1] Von Kuhl, pp. 70-80.
[2] Reflections on the World War, p. 132.

the German Army would be obliged to attack France through Belgium, and stipulated:

"The French Army could concentrate as rapidly as the German Army, and that as from the twelfth day it is in a position to take the offensive against Germany with *the help of the British Army on its left flank*."

And thus clearly outlines the co-operation agreed upon between Russia, France and Great Britain:

"It is essential that Germany shall be attacked at the same time on the east and on the west."

But the most important light is thrown upon the matter by the preamble in the minutes of the meetings of the French and Russian chiefs of staffs, which is here repeated:

PREAMBLE

The two chiefs of staff declare, by common accord, that the words "defensive war" must not be interpreted in the sense of a war which would be conducted defensively. They affirm, on the contrary, the absolute necessity for the Russian and French armies to adopt a vigorous offensive, and, as far as possible, a simultaneous one, in conformity with the text of Article 3 of the convention, whose terms provide that the forces of the two contracting powers shall come into full action with all speed.

The Franco-Russian Treaty, of 1892, provided "In case the forces of the Triple Alliance or of one of the powers which are a party to it" (for example, Austria) "should be mobilized, France and Russia, at the first indication of the event and without a previous agreement being necessary shall mobilize all their forces immediately and simultaneously and

shall transport them as near to their frontiers as possible."
* * * "These forces shall begin complete action with the
greatest dispatch, so that Germany will have to fight at the
same time in the east and in the west."

Therefore, when Austria partially mobilized for a local
war against Serbia in ignorance of the terms of this secret
Franco-Russian Treaty of 1892, Russia and France were
under a secret contract to mobilize immediately and attack
Germany with all their forces. *This was a secret declaration of war on Germany as of the date of the Austrian
mobilization, July 28, 1914, under the secret contract between
Russia and France of 1892 as modified finally by Poincaré
and Isvolski who had agreed on making the Austrian Serbian
war a basis for the general European war.*

The Russian and French mobilizations, which were begun
under the treaty of 1892, must be interpreted in the light
of that treaty and the annual military conferences from 1903
to 1913 of the general staffs of the Russian and French
armies.

The fact that Austria's mobilization was local and partial
and only against Serbia under terrible provocation made no
difference to the Russian and French conspirators. The
technical case of *casus foederis* had arisen and they instantly
took advantage of it.

The mobilization by Russia on July 30, 1914 under the
Franco-Russian contract of 1892 required the immediate invasion of Germany. The evidence is complete.

VII. Absence of a War Program in Germany

The German leaders have been painted in America and throughout the world as having brought on the World War. It was said that they had been preparing for this war for forty years; that they had been drinking to the day when they would launch it. Their extraordinary intellectual attainments were well known, their intelligence was conceded and it is impossible to believe that with no adequate object and with no treaties with other nations that were of any great value, they were proposing to fight the whole world. They were encircled on land and sea, and without raw materials, with foes outnumbering them overwhelmingly, and yet not only were they charged with planning the war with Russia, with France, with Belgium, with Great Britain, with Servia, Roumania, Japan, but with doing so knowing that they would not have the support even of Italy, and with Austria, their only reliable ally, seething with the Pan Slav movement and threatened with internal dissolution. Germany had everything to lose and nothing to gain, because it is inconceivable that the 300,000,000 people in Europe and the hundreds of millions outside of Europe, controlled by Great Britain, Russia, France and Japan would permit Germany to dominate Europe or the world. The theory that the German leaders willed the war violates every element of reason and common sense, and would require proof of the highest character to demonstrate that their leadership was so foolish as to will this war.

Sir Edward Goschen, British Ambassador to Berlin in 1914, wrote Nicolson on July 30, 1914, that he was firmly convinced that the German civil government and industrial and commercial leaders were strongly against war.

Professor Gooch, a leading English historian, in his book "Germany" says:

"No evidence has appeared to indicate that the German Government or the German people had desired and plotted a world war."

Honorable John S. Ewart, a leading jurist of Canada, in his "Roots and Causes of the Wars" fully confirms Professor Gooch.

Professor Harry Elmer Barnes in his comprehensive history, "The Genesis of the World War", sustains this view with overwhelming evidence.

A series of prominent French historians agree to the substantial facts. Among these are Pierre Renouvin in his book, "The Immediate Origin of the War"; M. Mathias Morhardt, distinguished French publicist, in his books, "The Proofs", "The Diplomatic Crime", etc.; and Georges Demartial, who says:

"We are convinced that we can no more accept the thesis of divided responsibility than we can accept that of the exclusive responsibility of Germany."

Gustave Dupin in his work, "Lecture on the Responsibility of the War," arrived at a like conclusion.

Sazonoff, the former Minister of Foreign Affairs, who was the chief conspirator, next to Isvolski, personally responsible for engineering this war, has confessed the complete authenticity of the official dispatches published in Un Livre Noir and by DeSiebert, which prove that a few Russian, Serbian and French leaders willed this War, and engineered it into action.

Finally, M. Raymond Poincaré, who, with Isvolski and Sazonoff, willed the war and actively incited the Russians to the general mobilization which began the war, makes the following confession in his apology printed in "Foreign Affairs," October, 1925:

"I do not claim that Austria or Germany in this first phase had a conscious thought-out intention of provoking a general war. No existing documents give us the right to suppose that at that time they had planned anything so systematic."

But this fatal admission by Poincaré is an absolute confession of the utter falsehood of the Entente propaganda in the United States that Germany had for years planned the World War, and brought it on.

The world does not need the admissions of Sazonoff or the confessions of Raymond Poincaré. The official proof is overwhelming that the Germans did not will the World War; that the Austrians did not will the World War; that the leaders of Serbia, of Russia and a very, very few French leaders, controlling nevertheless French Foreign Affairs, did will the World War. The evidence is complete and is not equivocal.

The absence of official evidence against Germany, the overwhelming evidence that the German Government tried to prevent a general war is in accord with the common sense reason that it was entirely against the German interest.

It is worth while to examine the Entente and Austro-German war preparations.

General Von Moltke, in his summary of 1912, says that Germany would be obliged, in the event of war, to take the field against France with an inferiority in infantry (though still with a slight superiority in artillery), and would further be attacked in the rear by Russia.

And he says:

"In view of the enormous sums Russia is spending on the reorganization of her army she will be stronger with every year that passes. It is just as impossible for Germany to try to compete with Russia as a land power as it is for her to attempt to catch up with England as a sea power."

In Chapter 10 [1] Bausman points out the preparedness of the Entente Allies—Russia, France and England—and that for 1914 the appropriations of Russia, France and England for war purposes made a total of $1,337,259,735, while Germany and Austria for 1914 appropriated $420,133,850, so that the Entente Allies appropriated $917,000,000 more in 1914 than Germany and Austria, and this does not include Belgium, Italy, Japan or the Balkans.

The number of men available for quick action in Russia and France alone was over 3,500,000, not counting their allies. The total for Germany and Austria was 1,176,741.

General Joffre in the Franco-Russian conference of 1913

---

[1] Let France Explain.

said he would have 200,000 more men than agreed to, that is, 1,500,00 men for immediate action.

Of course, Great Britain, France and Russia controlled the sea through the giant navy of Great Britain, and therefore Germany was cut off from supplies throughout the world, and its merchant marine and world commerce were destroyed at once, while the Entente Allies had the whole world to draw from.

When the war ended Germany, with approximately 67,-000,000 people, was facing nearly the whole world, or over 1,400,000,000 people, allied or associated with the Entente Powers.

Chancellor Hollweg states that:

"The supposition that Germany let loose war out of mere lust of world power is so silly that a historian would only take it seriously in the entire absence of any other explanation at all. * * * Such an assumption ascribes to us the sort of folly that is only attributed to an opponent in the heat of political controversy."[1]

He says with moderation and justice:

"The controversy as to which party gave the first impulse to a program of general armament and to a perversion of the policy of alliances will probably never be fought to a finish. Immeasurable mutual distrust, imperialistic ideals, and a patriotism restricted to material national instincts respectively worked each other up without its ever being possible to say that any particular nation had contributed most to the general tendency of the world."[2]

[1] Hollweg, 163.
[2] Hollweg, 169.

Hollweg points out that Russia mobilized because it desired war. It refused to suspend mobilization,

"In spite of the fact that Vienna was ready to enter into direct conversation with Petersburg on the Serbian issue.

"In spite of the fact that Vienna had accepted the Grey mediation.

"In spite of the fact that Vienna had given assurances as to the integrity of Serbia.

"In spite of the fact that Vienna was prepared not to go beyond such a temporary occupation of a part of Serbian territory as England itself had considered acceptable.

"Finally, in spite of the fact that Austria had only mobilized against Serbia, and that Germany had not yet mobilized at all."

Former Chancellor Hollweg then says:

"Consequently, when the telegraph brought us news of the mobilization on the morning of the 31st of July, we could not be other than convinced that Russia desired war under all conditions."

It appears that neither Germany nor Austria knew the terms of the treaty of 1892 requiring Russia and France to attack Germany if Austria mobilized. Indeed the people of Russia, of France, of Belgium, of Great Britain did not know of it.

The German leaders thought they had artillery superior to the French. As a matter of fact, the heavy artillery of Germany was better, but the French field gun recoiled on an air cushion, multiplying the speed of the gun without making it necessary to resight it—a fact of great importance in maintaining a barrage. This wonderful gun was greatly superior to the German guns in speed and accuracy.

The Russian preparations for this war were gigantic and

the manner in which they worked out the detail of military and railway preparations is set forth by Von Eggeling in "The Russian Mobilization and the Outbreak of the War", and by General H. von Kuhl,[1] showing gross force of 2,292,-000 men.[2] The peace strength in the summer of 1914 was 1,581,000 officers and men. The war strength was 3,461,-750 men.[3] The evidence shows that Grand Duke Nicholas insisted on war in 1912. Sukhomlinoff, Chief of Staff, opposed on the ground that they were not yet ready.[4] In the spring of 1914 the Duma sanctioned increases equal to the entire peace strength of the Austrian and Hungarian armies. Continual test mobilizations were made, supplies were imported, coal reserves increased, rolling stock added, grain export was stopped. In the autumn of 1913 General Joffre headed a military mission to St. Petersburg to examine the Russian military efficiency, and remarked:

"The Russian army is at this moment the mightiest in the world."

The German General Staff believed that the Russian field forces of the first line could be ready on the fifth day of mobilization, and the second line on the eighth day. The German leaders did not dare to wait longer.

General Dobrorolski, in charge of Russian mobilization, estimated the general mobilization would call to the colors 14,000,000 men.

[1] See Exhibit 10, Congressional Record, 391.

[2] Von Kuhl, 61.

[3] Von Kuhl, 104.

[4] Eggeling, 49-50.

It is not surprising that when William II was advised by the Czar that steps for mobilization had been in progress five days on July 29th, he demanded a cessation of the mobilization with the statement that otherwise he would be compelled to mobilize. He begged the Czar to stop it and warned him if the menace to Germany continued the Czar would be entirely responsible for the war. The Czar immediately afterwards reordered general mobilization.

Poincaré's acknowledgment that Germany had made various overtures to France to establish a rapprochement with a view to maintaining European peace, may be taken at its full value. The cold-blooded refusal of the French leaders to permit this friendly rapprochement shows that the leaders in the Quai d'Orsay had the determined purpose of carrying out the contract of 1892 with Russia, and the military conventions, and had the will to war.

Even Isvolski, in his memoirs, narrates the great personal efforts of William II, in 1905, to establish permanent peace between Russia, Germany and France in the so-called treaty of Bjorkoe, pledging Russia and Germany to a treaty of mutual defensive security, in which Article 4 provided:

"When this treaty goes into effect, Russia will take the necessary steps to make its terms known to France, and invite her to subscribe to it as an ally."

Not only did the statesmen in charge of the French Foreign Office refuse to concur, but they demanded the cancellation of this agreement between Russia and Germany,

which, of course, was a contradiction of the agreement between France and Russia to attack Germany in a certain contingency, which both the French and Russian statesmen knew
could be compelled when they were prepared for the physical conflict, that is, the "mobilization" of Austria. It is un-
necessary to give the details of the various efforts made by
the German Government, because the will to war on the
part of the Russian and French leaders has been fully proven
with all Germany's evidence entirely omitted. What is the
need of German witnesses when overwhelming evidence is
available from the Entente records and witnesses of the
highest order from the nations opposing Germany?

VIII. THE SECRET DISPATCHES OF THE RUSSIAN FOREIGN OFFICE

Innumerable secret dispatches passing between the Russian Foreign Office and the Russian Ambassadors at Paris
and at London, Isvolski and Benckendorff, set forth the
policy of the Russian leaders to bring about a general European war for the purpose of getting control of the Dardanelles. These dispatches prove they intrigued to bring the
war about and bring Great Britain into it without British
opinion knowing the Russian purpose or the Russian responsibility, but aimed to make the public, both in Great Britain
and in France, as well as in the world at large, believe that the
World War was due to German aggression. On January 29,

1913, Isvolski telegraphed the Russian Foreign Office immediately after Poincaré's election as President, as follows:[1]

"I have just had a long conversation with Poincaré, who has declared to me in his capacity as President of the Republic he will have
abundant possibility of directly influencing the foreign policy of
France. * * * According to him it is of the highest importance for
the French Government to be able in advance to take part in directing
public opinion as to a war which could arise in the matter of the
Balkans."[2] * * * *

And on January 30, 1913;[3]

"The energy, the decision, and the entire character of M. Poincaré
appears to the guaranty of that which in his capacity as President
of the Republic he will not content himself—as, for example, M.
Faïlierès—with a role purely passive and, if it might be so expressed,
decorative, but that he would influence by every means and at all
times the French policy in the domain of foreign affairs.* * * That
is why during the next seven years we can be completely assured
against the appearance at the head of the French Government and
diplomacy of such persons as Caillaux, Cruppi, Nonis, etc. * * *
M. Poincaré continues to come every day to the ministry, and M.
Jonnert (Minister of Foreign Affairs) makes no reply, expresses no
opinion without he has knowledge of it and consents to it. * * *"

"The French Government is firmly decided to fulfill toward us its
obligation as an ally, and it admits with full knowledge and with all
the cold blood necessary that the final result of the actual complications can be for it the necessity of the participation of France in a
general war. The moment when France should draw the sword is
exactly determined by the Franco-Russian military convention and

[1] "Un Livre Noir," p. 14, etc.
[2] Congressional Record, 364.
[3] Un Livre Noir, Vol. II, pages 19-20.

under the understanding the French ministry entertain not the slightest doubt nor the slightest hesitation. * * *

"Also the French Government does not wish to deprive Russia of its liberty of action, nor to put in doubt the moral obligations which rest upon it in that which concerns the Balkan States. Consequently Russia can count not only on the support in arms of France in the case foreseen by the Franco-Russian convention but upon the most energetic and effective diplomatic assistance (of France) in all the enterprises of the Russian Government in favor of said States (the Balkans)."

This official record convicts the Russian and French leaders. The original contract to attack Germany was being steadily worked out by the conspirators.

Poincaré undertook his own defense by writing a book, "Les Origines de la Guerre" in 1921, (in English 1922), an analysis of which appears in "Let France Explain", Chapter XIV. He wholly omits the Russian mobilization and does not contradict the Belgian minister's charge against him as responsible for bringing on the war. He omits the vital record of the falsification of the Russian Orange Book and the French Yellow Book, but admits:

"(a) That the Kaiser made repeated efforts to come to a good understanding with France (p. 25).

"(b) That Delcassé made a revision, which he misquotes, of the Franco-Russian treaty (p. 56).

"(c) That France had always in mind the recovery of the lost Provinces (p. 25).

"(d) That the Franco-Russian treaty (of 1892) was never disclosed before the war and that Viviani, with a copy in his pocket, refrained from reading it to the Parliament.

"(e) That the pacific Georges Louis (French Ambassador) was

recalled from St. Petersburg because the Russians wanted a different sort." [1]

Poincaré's defense will be found in the "Living Age", Saturday, August 26, 1922, page 503, in which he says that Sazonoff, who plotted the war, was a "pacifist".

He was, on the contrary, with Isvolski, a Pan-Slavic and Greek Orthodox fanatic, and the man who deliberately planned the European War while always artfully trying to make himself appear blameless. The war strategy was to put the moral odium on Germany.

Poincaré says: "The thought of crushing Serbia dominated the whole policy of Austria and Germany," and he affected as deep concern about Serbia as did Sazonoff. It was a pretext for a desired war. He said that when he and Viviani (July 29, 1914) "reached Paris we were received by a *startled and troubled nation* that, *far from wishing war,* was *overwhelmed with solicitude for the safety of France,* although firmly resolved upon *any sacrifices to defend the fatherland.*" That is what most of the French people thought, but Poincaré was resolved on a war of aggression, not of defense.

That very night, July 29th, Poincaré, Viviani and the Minister of War met and definitely decided on war. Two nights later—July 31st—the French Minister of War told the military attaché of the Russian Embassy with "enthusiastic sincerity" that "the French Government is firmly decided upon war" and requested the Russian Embassy to

[1] "Let France Explain," p. 229.

confirm the hope of the French General Staff that all the Russian efforts should be directed against Germany. (Telegram 216.)

Poincaré states that with the consent of the ministry he wrote a letter to King George on July 31, 1914, informing the King that France would do all in her power to maintain peace. This letter to King George is flatly contradicted by Telegram 216, is inconsistent with the contract of 1892, with the secret military agreement to attack Germany, with the secret conferences of the Russian and French General Staffs of 1911, of 1912, and of 1913 (approved of Poincaré) to mobilize and attack Germany in the event of an Austrian mobilization. But Poincaré's hypocritical letter was extremely serviceable in convincing British public opinion of the peaceful attitude of the French Government and of the guilt of the German Government in willing the war. His letter to the king was a "ruse de guerre".

Asquith, on Saturday, August 1st, at 2 A.M., had King George telegraph to the Czar, making a strong appeal for peace. (See page 1 N. Y. Times, August 2, 1914.) Asquith and King George knew well to whom to appeal. It was to the Czar, the authority responsible for making the war, and not to the German Kaiser, that King George appealed.

This fact has great significance.

King George then wired the Czar in behalf of peace, after the Russian and French Governments were fully committed to war, and Great Britain bound to follow. It was a graceful and useful gesture and went far to satisfy public opinion, that Great Britain did not wish the war and tried to prevent it. Of course the war was already launched and Grey, Poincaré and Sazonoff knew it.

Poincaré insisted on having *Grey announce the Entente,* avowedly as a means of preventing Germany from declaring war. Grey was unwilling, probably because *at that moment* it would have offended British public opinion, which was not advised of Grey's secret commitments to France, much less to Russia. Grey's commitment to France had been repeatedly denied by Grey and his representatives.

Grey had no option but to support France in the war when it came (and however it came) with Germany because of his commitments, but above all because of his conviction of what was to Great Britain's interest.

On the night of July 29, the British Ambassador at Berlin wired Sir Edward Grey that the German Chancellor had told him (the British Ambassador in Berlin) that: "As far as he was able to judge the main principle which governed British policy was that Great Britain would never stand by and allow France to be crushed in any conflict there might be." [1]

So that it is clear that the German Government expected Great Britain to support France in the event of war. The fact that the Russians knew Great Britain would support France fully justified the Russian war party and the French war party in their determination on war, and justified the German leaders in doing their utmost to prevent war.

[1] "How Diplomats Make War," 263.

Moreover, Sir Edward Grey told the French Ambassador at London, Cambon,[1] that he meant to tell the German Ambassador that day, Wednesday, July 29, that he must not be misled from the friendly tone of their conversation that Britain would stand aside, so that both Germany and France knew that Britain would not stand aside. When Germany fought she knew she had overwhelming odds against her.

On Friday, July 31, the British Ambassador to Berlin, Sir Edward Goschen, wired Sir Edward Grey that the German Chancellor said he had done everything possible to attain his object at Vienna, but he could not leave his country defenseless *"while time was being utilized by other powers; and if, as he learns is the case, military measures are now being taken by Russia against Germany also, it will be impossible for him to remain quiet."* [2]

Sir Edward Grey telegraphed to the British Ambassador at St. Petersburg that he did not see how Russia could be urged to suspend military preparations unless some limit were put by Austria to the advance of her troops into Serbia.[3]

In other words, he did not exercise a moderating influence on St. Petersburg; he justified their military preparedness, although he knew Austria was not threatening Russia and had no intention of taking Serb territory or impairing its sovereignty.

The whole story is set forth quite fully by Neilson, for-

[1] British White Paper, 87.

[2] Ibid., 281.

[3] Ibid., 282.

merly a member of the British Parliament, in Chapter 12 of "How Diplomats Make War." The chapter is entitled, "A Game of Chess".

Colonel E. M. House, in 1913 and 1914, sensing the possibility of war in Europe, made a resolute effort to bring about a peaceful understanding between Great Britain, France and Germany. He had intimate contact with the British leaders and the French leaders, as the trusted representative of the President of the United States.

He went to London and Paris, urged upon the British and French leaders an understanding between them and Germany, and went to Berlin, where his suggestion met with a friendly reception. He made no real progress with the British or French in his efforts to prevent war.

On May 29, 1914, he wrote the President of the United States the following prophetic words:

"Whenever England consents, France and Russia will close in on Germany and Austria."

Within seventy-five days England had openly *consented,* had itself declared war on Germany, and Russia and France had taken the concrete steps to *close in on Germany and Austria* as House said they would do.

But instantly Germany, completely blockaded, was strenuously advertised in a world-wide campaign as being exclusively guilty of launching the War. The falsehood was believed and became the corner-stone of the Versailles

Treaty (Article 231). The peace of the peoples of Europe cannot safely rest on this dangerous foundation.

Without doubt patriotism in the form of intense nationalism moved most of the European leaders, who thought in terms of military strategy alone.

It is futile to reproach individuals in the foreign offices of St. Petersburg, of Paris or of London. These men were produced by their environment in an atmosphere of secret diplomacy, believing in the power of might first, last and all the time, but nevertheless also believing it necessary to subsidize the press and direct public opinion so as to have the support as far as possible of their own nationals.

A profound distrust between the leaders of the different nations was everywhere evident.

These foreign offices were controlled by a consuming desire for further political power over other people and over other territory. Their whole diplomacy in foreign relations largely consisted of trading with each other, giving and taking "compensations". The prime moving force was commercialized imperialism.

One of the most convincing evidences of the conscious war responsibility of the Russian Foreign Office is the wholesale falsification of the Russian Orange Book, in which out of sixty dispatches immediately preceding the war fifty of them were falsified by striking out items that would demonstrate that the Russian or French leaders willed the war or that the Germans or Austrians did not will the war. The fol-

lowing telegrams show some of these falsifications. The
words now appearing in italics *were stricken out* in the Russian Orange Book and in some cases other words were inserted.   (See Chapter IV. Section V.)

These corrected Russian dispatches prove that the Germans and Austrians did not will the general European war
and that the Russian and French leaders in control did will
it.

IX. The European Press

The press of Russia, Germany, France, and Serbia in
1914 was a press largely controlled by subsidies.

The journals were not supported by advertisements as in
America.   They relied upon subsidies from governments,
politicians, and from commercial and financial interests.

Through such agencies the people of Germany, France
and Russia were taught to hate each other. The death of the
crown prince of Austria was attributed by the Government
of Austria to the Serbian press propaganda financed by the
Russian Government through the Russian Minister at Belgrade with the connivance of the Serbian Government.   In
Livre Noir, which discloses the secret archives of the Russian Foreign Office, are many dispatches showing the manner
in which the Russian Government subsidized and directed
the press.

On page 208, Livre Noir, Vol. II. for example, in telegram 591, December 18, 1913, Isvolski, the Russian Ambassador at Paris, speaking of the Paris press, says:

"The papers which are devoted to us, as Le Matin, rely on me for instructions, and if we do not give them directions they might perhaps engage themselves with a false view."

On page 213 (ibid.) Isvolski says:

"It is particularly important here, at such a moment, to control the press. Otherwise it may engage itself with a false view; besides it is more than sure that it is continually moved by financial circles who have in view only their own special interests."

On page 371 of Vol. II. Isvolski writes:

"Endeavoring to maintain the attitudes which are desirable for us with the press of the government and political world, I am doing my utmost at the same time to influence the press. With this in view, thanks to the measures taken in time, considerable results have been obtained. As you know, I do not intervene directly in the distribution of the subsidies, but this distribution in which the French ministers take part, the Minister of Foreign Affairs and the Minister of Finance, is, it appears, efficacious and obtains its ends. From my side I exert myself every day to influence personally the most important journals of Paris such as Temps, Journal des Debats, L'Echo de Paris."

Hundreds of thousands of francs of Russian money were paid monthly to the French press by the lieutenants of Poincaré.

The manner in which the press responded to such stimulation has heretofore been shown in the dispatches quoted, showing that the newspapers were potent instrumentalities in moving the French and Russian people to war.

From these disclosures it will appear how extremely significant to the German rulers was the attitude of the French press in Paris in July, 1914, when they were denouncing Germany and Austria and demanding the support of Russia, and it is worthwhile to recall the declaration of the "Nouvelle Revue" that France was determined on war, and of the Petrograd press that Russia was determined on war, and that France and Russia were prepared.

The attitude of the French war party may be appreciated from the quotation of Mr. Buxton, in the Foreign Office debate of July, 1912, taken from the "Nouvelle Revue", one of the most prominent of Paris periodicals :[1]

"We intend to have war. After 40 years of a heavily armed peace we can at least utter this opinion without the serious readers of a French revue shaking in their shoes. * * * France is ready to strike, and to conquer, as she was not ready 40 years ago, and as she will not be in four or five years to come, owing to the annual divergent numbers of the birth rate in each country. * * * We, the *attacking party,* will have arranged with England that their fleet * * * will have followed * * * the remains of the whole German Navy into the German waters."

X. BRIBERY OF THE FRENCH PRESS

On March 16, 1909, Isvolski, in a long letter to the Russian Foreign Office, used the following language :

"*The French Government* fully realizes the extent of its obligations into which it entered towards us and *will fulfill its duty* at the moment when the national honor of Russia in Serbia is pledged against Austria—but how will the French people take it? Will they

[1] How Diplomats Make War, p. 206.

find satisfaction in seeing peace endangered by Serbia and *in the prospect of war against Germany?"*

In other words the French Foreign Office pledged France to fight with Russia against Germany when the local war between Austria and Serbia under the Russian promise of co-operation to Serbia should begin and furnish the pretext. But the attitude of the French people was a question. That question was settled by subsidizing the French press and making the people or their leaders believe France had a vital interest in the local Austro-Serb controversy.

And since the socialist and radical press was especially hostile to any war because of the Balkans, Isvolski took the steps necessary to influence the French press by the use of Russian money, which was steadily kept up, as will appear from the following sample telegrams:

"Strictly confidential.

July 8-21, 1912.

No. 348.

"Dear Sergei Dimitrievitch:

"From this interview I was convinced that *M. Poincaré is in every respect in accord with us, considers the moment has finally arrived to realize the century-old aims of our traditional policy (the seizure of the Straits) and therewith restore the European balance of power by the return of the stolen provinces of Alsace-Lorraine.*

"Poincaré did not conceal the great difficulties which we have to overcome yet. The principal trouble he expects from the radical Socialists *who are opposed to any war caused by financial or commercial reasons, especially when its origin is in the Balkans.* This party has some highly intelligent men: Caillaux, Herriot, Painlevé, and disposes of a considerable number of deputies and newspapers.

Of the latter, some have only a few readers—Le Radical, La Lanterne, Le Rappel, L'Action, L'Aurore, La Depeche de Toulouse—but they have much influence. They are the mouthpiece of some prominent leader and accorded by his partisans unflinching political obedience. Each of these publishers and leaders is backed by a group of deputies and senators who want to rise with him and submit themselves without contradiction * * * *M. Poincaré shares my opinion that a very large sacrifice on our part is necessary for this purpose.* I hardly dare to mention the amount—*three million francs*—of which 250,000 francs alone is for the Radical, the organ of Senator Perchot. If we consider that *the Turkish Government* has spent *five millions* to *influence the French press* and *bought* even one of their most prominent authors (Pierre Loti) and if we also contemplate the *relative insignificance* of this amount *in comparison to the world-changing program* which we can bring closer to realization therewith, you may want to undertake to submit this proposition to the cabinet for their immediate consent.

"I propose that the subsidy be paid in monthly installments *as heretofore* in order to be sure every minute *of the zeal of the newspapers.* I consider it advantageous this time not to use Lenoir but Laffon. Laffon has considerable influence with the Matin, whose financial director he was, as well as with the great dailies.

Isvolski."

This communication printed in "Behind the Scenes in French Journalism" was identified under oath by former Prime Minister Kokovtzev in the libel suit of the Matin against Humanité.

To the telegram of July 8-21, Sazonoff replied:

July 13-28, 1912.

"In consequence of your excellency's letter of July 8-21 (No. 348) I have not failed to submit your proposition and the report of your conversation to the cabinet, *presided over by His Majesty.* It is a great joy to be able to communicate to you that the request of the

President of the Republic regarding the amounts to be put by us at the disposition of the press, has, after some natural hesitations (quelques hesitations bien comprehensibles), *been granted by His Majesty* with the condition that, *as heretofore,* Privy Councillor Raffalowitch will be entrusted with the financial part of the transaction. The State Counselor Davidoff will start for Paris immediately with the most far-reaching instructions."

So the Czar authorized it.

The matter was put in the hands of Raffalowitch, who, on the 30th of November, 1912, wired for *additional* finances for secret distribution in Paris. A number of such demands were made.

To the Russian Foreign Minister was sent the following telegram:

"October 10-23, 1912.

"Some time ago I wrote to you, as well as to Kokovzeff, about the absolute necessity of *providing further funds* for the purpose of influencing the French press.

"As I personally have very little experience in such matters, I conferred with Privy Councillor Raffalowitch, who is familiar with such questions and who proposes the following scheme: To immediately provide for that purpose Frs. 300,000—and to entrust Lenoir with the distribution as the latter has managed *previous distributions.* It is very important not to undertake anything without consulting Poincaré. French statesmen are practised in such matters and possess incredible adroitness.

ISVOLSKI."

Sazonoff complied October 17th, and authorized Departmental Chief Davidoff to act. Davidoff sent Sazonoff the following wire:

"October 17-30, 1912.

"Summary of my conference with Poincaré and ambassador. *Further* credit 300,000 for quick *press-intervention* as soon as same becomes necessary. This is reasonable and I accepted subject to referring to your Excellency."

This system was kept up, and on November 7, 1913, (for one of many examples), Raffalowitch reported to the Russian Ministry the following disbursements:

La Lanterne	Frs. 42,000	Millerand's paper
L'Aurore	" 17,000	Clemenceau's paper
L'Evenement	" 11,000	
L'Action	" 9,000	
La France	" 11,000	
Le Rappel	" 7,000	
Le Gil Blas	" 2,000	
Le Journal	" 1,000	

and on November 19, 1913, he reported the following disbursements:

Le Radical	Frs. 120,000	
La Lanterne	" 35,000	Millerand's paper
Le Figaro	" 25,000	
Le Temps	" 50,000	
La Libre Parole	" 80,000	
L'Aurore	" 45,000	Clemenceau's paper
Le Gaulois	" 25,000	
La Liberté	" 30,000	

Raffalowitch made the following communication to Isvolski:

"December 11, 1912.

"I have already informed your Excellency that Lenoir at the instigation of Klotz, who herein is Poincaré's mouthpiece, has pledged
himself firmly towards the journals, 'L'Aurore,' 'Lanterne,' 'Radical,'
etc.—as well as to certain directors of journals having but small
editions, but great influence in politics."

It was under these subsidies of the French press that the
French people were worked up by special writers to believe
that it was the interest of France to support Russia in defending Serbia on the pretense of maintaining "the balance
of power" in the Balkans, while Russian money in Serbia
had excited the intrigues of Serbia, which led to the assassination of numerous Austrian officials (finally of the Grand
Duke Ferdinand) and compelled Austria to mobilize against
Serbia in self-protection. This local act of war of Austria
against Serbia was used then as a pretext for Russian general mobilization, which really meant a secret declaration
of war by Russia and France against Germany, as shown
by the contract of 1892-4, the military conferences, and the
secret dispatches already published.

The book "Behind the Scenes of French Journalism" tells
how the press was used by French officials to influence the
whole world by false propaganda, as opinion in Paris, St.
Petersburg and Serbia had been influenced.

Three days before the war broke out, a resolution was
offered and passed the same day, by the French Parliament,
providing 25,000,000 francs for the establishment of the
"Maison de la Presse". The House of the Press was a
building of 200 rooms, No. 3 Rue Francois, five stories

high, where the war news was distributed, propaganda manufactured, photographs of well-painted atrocities made to prove the wickedness of the Germans; the usual war lies circulated. There were 80 employees transmitting to the Foreign Press, *free of charge,* and in eighteen civilized languages, reports of French victories and painted cruelties of the Huns and Boches. Here was distributed the amiable stories about the Germans cutting off the hands of children, crucifying prisoners, boiling their own dead for fat, etc. (Supra)

They lived up to the language of Isvolski, and showed "incredible adroitness".

The British lie factory was not far behind. Unity of Chicago of Mar. 7, 1927, quotes Rt. Hon. Arthur Ponsonby as to how the films were made in England for use in America to change a pacifist into a militarist. The story of the Germans boiling their *own* dead for fat and glycerine was an English invention. The Lusitania medals representing the Germans celebrating the sinking of the Lusitania were made in England. The pictures of cheering Germans about the Kaiser's Palace celebrating the sinking of the Lusitania was an English fake.

Unhappily war lies freely circulated among all of the belligerents. There were none who were innocent of these wrongs.

CHAPTER IV

HOW RUSSIA AND
FRANCE FORCED WAR
IN 1914

I. THE WILL TO WAR

In ascertaining "the will to war," it is of the greatest importance to study these dispatches and to consider the true intent as indicated by their language, the context, the secret treaties and conferences of the General Staffs of Russia, France and Great Britain.

It is clear from these dispatches that the Russian Imperialists, in pursuance of the contract they made with the French President in 1892 to attack Germany, had persistently for 22 years maintained a fixed policy of attacking Germany when the time arrived at which it could be done with a certainty of success; that they had borrowed billions of money from France with which to prepare for the day; that they had carried on their secret military conferences, and had the machinery of war completely worked out with the most modern methods of inter-communication by messenger, telegraph, telephone and by wireless.

It is perfectly clear that the object of the conspiracy was

the control of the Dardanelles, over-lordship of the Balkans, the acquisition of Austrian and German territory, and making the Romanoff Dynasty the over-lord of Eastern Europe, and by breaking down the power of Germany and Austria, giving it a position of greatly increased power in the world.

The manner of accomplishing this conspiracy is equally clear. It was to be done by a policy of complete encirclement of Germany, by disorganizing Austria with a Pan-Slav movement, alienating Italy by secret promises, and striking Germany with a sudden over-powering blow. Germany was to be kept entirely in the dark with regard to this conspiracy.

Nicholas, in pursuance of this design, invited William II to act as a mediator between Russia and Austria, thereby to allay apprehensions that would otherwise be aroused by the Russian mobilization. The mobilization was to be rushed, and the German Emperor kept in ignorance of its significance until it was too late.

The proposals for adjusting the difficulties between Austria, Serbia and Russia by international conferences, was a ruse of war intended to keep the German leaders quiet until a sledge-hammer blow could be suddenly delivered.

Consider, for instance, Telegram 210 of July 30, 1914, in which Isvolski, the Russian Ambassador at Paris, told Sazonoff, the Russian Minister of Foreign Affairs, that the French War Minister had advised the Russian Military Attache that—

*"we could declare that in the higher interests of peace we are
ready to delay our preparations for mobilization since this would not
prevent us from continuing our preparations, and indeed from inten-
sifying them, but we should have to refrain from the possible greater
movements of troops."*

And on the night of July 31, 1914, Dispatch No. 216
showed a determined purpose to war by the French Government, though in the meantime and thereafter, the Minister
of Foreign Affairs of France was assuring the German Ambassador at Paris that they were trying to work out a
friendly adjustment, and on July 31 Sazonoff was sending
out dispatches pretending that he wanted a peaceful adjustment, although fully committed to war.

In the meantime both Paris and London refused to exercise any moderating influence on St. Petersburg. St. Petersburg notified Paris and London that it would not submit
to moderating influences while Berlin was doing its utmost to
exercise a moderating influence in Vienna and succeeded.
The Russian leaders would not have refused to listen unless
they had been already assured that this attitude would be
acceptable to Paris and London. It was a part of the plot.

August 1, 1914, Telegram No. 233, Poincaré told Isvolski
that—

*"during the last few days the Austrian Ambassador had energeti-
cally assured him and Viviani that Austria had declared to Russia her
readiness not only to respect the territorial integrity of Serbia, but
also her sovereign rights, but that Russia had intentionally concealed
these assurances."*

Austria made the same representations to London, but, of course, they were unavailing because the Imperial Russian conspirators had no intention whatever of permitting Germany and Austria to escape. They were determined to have the war for which they had made such long and careful preparations, and from which they entertained such high hopes of great glory and power.

II. JULY 24, 1914

July 24, 1914, presents a complete demonstration that the Allies anticipated a general European war and were taking full steps to that end, and that Germany was not anticipating a European war.

On July 24, 1914, there was no pretense whatever that any steps looking to war were being taken by the German Government.

On July 24, 1914, Serbia's preparation of a reply to Austria's demand for redress and security was being accompanied by plans for an immediate mobilization of all of her army, under the secret understanding with Russia.

On July 24, 1914, the Russian Crown Council made plans for mobilization, and Januskewitch, Chief of Staff under Sukhomlinoff, gave the order to General Dobrorolski, officer in charge of mobilization, to prepare for the mobilization of 1,100,000 Russian troops.

This was a secret declaration of war against Germany, in strict pursuance of the secret treaty of 1892. It involved ultimately calling to the colors 14,000,000 men (Dobrorolski on Russian Mobilization). The official pretense that it was a partial mobilization was merely a piece of self-serving official hypocrisy, intended to prevent Germany from knowing it until too late to adequately defend. Sukhomlinoff on the 25th of July had dinner with Baron Rosen and on the receipt of a dispatch from Serbia that the Serbs had mobilized, exclaimed: "This time we shall march." He was Minister of War of Russia, and he knew and his testimony unconsciously given is of the first magnitude.

On July 24th Sazonoff said on receiving news of the Austrian ultimatum: "C'est la guerre Europeenne"—"this is the European war." [1]

Sazonoff, Minister of Foreign Affairs, in declaring he would not permit any moderating influence from the British or French Government, knew what the policy of Russia was —that it was for war. His pretense of favoring peace had no foundation of fact.

Boghitchevitch, who was the Diplomatic Representative of Serbia, in Paris up to 1907, and then at Berlin up to 1914, with regard to Sazonoff's self-serving public expression that the war had been made too soon in his opinion and at a time he thought not propitious, says: [2]

"The insincerity of the Minister was complete, but his hypocritical declarations succeeded in making him appear before the European cabinets as an adversary of Russian Pan-Slavism, of which he was

[1] Barnes, p. 200.
[2] "Les Causes de la Guerre," p. 69.

on the contrary—the course of events of the war of 1914 demonstrated it—the damned soul."

Boghitchevitch was quite right. Not only Sazonoff refused in advance to consider any moderating influence from Great Britain or France as to Russia's artificial, unfounded controversy with Austria as to Serbia, but Poincaré and Viviani, representing France, refused to try to exercise any moderating influence on the war policy of Sazonoff; and Edward Grey, representing Great Britain, also refused.

Boghitchevitch testifies strongly in his book (supra) to "The Will to War" of Serbia and Russia,[1] and says of Germany, that its decisions were inspired by the fixed purpose "to maintain peace". He says [2] "To fight Germany was the one reason which determined France to seek the alliance with Russia."

On July 24, 1914, the Belgian Foreign Office sent out a circular to Belgian officers, that Belgium was completely mobilized, although the official order of Belgian mobilization was not published until July 30, 1914. Again the public was deceived as to the time of Belgian mobilization.

On July 24, 1914, France ordered its African troops to France.

On July 24, 1914, France took preliminary steps for mobilizing and was ready for action in eleven days when Poincaré addressed the French Assembly on August 4, 1914; so

[1] Ibid., p. 107.
[2] Ibid., p. 111.

general mobilization must have started about July 24th, notwithstanding the delay in the publication of the announcement. The French and Russian leaders were intimately cooperating.

On July 24, 1914, France had already withdrawn its navy from the Atlantic seaboard to the Mediterranean, relying upon British protection.

On July 24, 1914, Poincaré and Viviani were on their way from St. Petersburg, Russia, where they had been received with great pomp and circumstance, and where they had renewed assurances to the Russian authorities that France was ready, and would support Russia in making war on Germany.[1] They reached Paris on July 29, and on the night of July 31st the famous Dispatch 216 from Isvolski to Sazonoff declared that the French War Minister had informed the Russian Military Attaché with enthusiastic sincerity that the French Government was firmly decided upon war, and expressed the hope that all the Russian efforts would be directed against Germany, and that Austria should be treated as a negligible quantity. According to the secret Franco-Russian conventions "the aggressor shall be the power which mobilizes first" (No. 53), and "mobilization is the declaration of war" (No. 71). Under the Franco-Russian Treaty and Annual Military Conventions the French and Russian mobilizations were to be followed by the immediate attack on Germany. The mobilization orders

[1] See Margueritte, "Les Criminels."

of France and Russia under the Treaty were absolutely equivalent to a secret declaration of war against Germany.

On July 24, 1914, Great Britain had its war fleet mobilized for war in control of the North Sea, the outlet of the Baltic, the English Channel and the French coast. On July 24, 1914, France had its entire war fleet ready for action in the Mediterranean Sea.

On July 24, 1914, William II, who had been painted by Allied propaganda as the monster who unchained the dogs of war, was quietly cruising the northern waters of the Baltic Sea on his summer vacation, apparently unconscious that his complete ruin was impending.

He came back on Sunday, the 26th of July, and immediately began his strenuous but useless appeals for European peace.

He had been grossly deceived by Nicholas II, who, with unbelievable hypocrisy, had asked him to intervene for peace as a mediator between Austria and Serbia, at the very time when a general mobilization was going on in Russia, with the well understood purpose of the Russian leaders immediately to attack Germany under the secret treaty of 1892. Even Sazonoff has written that the Kaiser begged the Czar to keep his troops from the border, and that William II was "nearly frantic".

The die was cast. The war was already in progress. The entire Entente mobilization was ready, and under full swing. The avalanche was grandly moving. The World War had begun. William II was wasting his breath.

III. The Case Against Poincaré

The secret record shows abundantly, from prominent witnesses in all the Entente countries, that neither the German nor the Austrian leaders had any purpose to bring on a European war. They did not will the war. The German leaders did their utmost to prevent it when they saw it threatened. The conspiracy of the Russian and a few French leaders willed the war, and deliberately brought it on for the purpose first set forth in the statement of this case.

It should be remembered that in England only Asquith, Edward Grey and very few others knew about Grey's secret commitments; John Burns, Lord Morley and others about August 1, 1914, withdrew from Asquith's Cabinet when they discovered the truth.

It should be remembered that the great body of the French leaders were as ignorant of the secret intrigues of Poincaré as the body of the French and English people were, for the secret treaty of 1892, to attack Germany was a profound state secret.

But Poincaré, Isvolski and Sazonoff thoroughly understood it and each other.

Poincaré wrapped himself in the cloak of France, and loudly proclaimed, "France does not wish war", and repeated and repeated such phrases, but peace-loving France was one thing, and Poincaré was another thing. Poincaré is not France, and happily France is not Poincaré. The French

people desired peace. Poincaré desired war, and engineered
the French people into a gigantic disaster. Even the people
of Alsace Lorraine were opposed to war ; the Diet of Alsace-
Lorraine had unanimously passed resolutions against war on
May 6, 1913. Poincaré expressed his true sentiments at the
University of Paris, October, 1920, when he said :

"I have not been able to see any other reason for my generation
living, except the hope of recovering our lost provinces."

Poincaré has so far failed to disprove the following serious
disclosures made against him by the evidence :

1. That he refused the German efforts at rapprochement
in 1912 and its offer of self-governing autonomy for Alsace-
Lorraine.

2. His agreement with Isvolski to support Russia in a war
arising over the Balkans which should bring in Germany.

3. The appointment of Delcassé and Paléologue as Ambassadors to Russia, knowing they favored war.

4. His participation in bribing the French press, with
Russian money to support Russia in the war breeding policy
in the Balkans.

5. The financing of the Russian Army and military railroads against Germany.

6. Promoting the Anglo-Russian Naval Convention in
spring of 1914.

7. His stimulation of the Russian War Party at St. Petersburg in the week preceding the Russian mobilization of July
1914, which launched the war.

8. Throwing his personal influence for war on the night of July 29, 1914, and allowing his Minister of War to advise Russia on the night of July 31, France was determined on war.

9. Withholding from the French people his commitments to Russia and deceiving them as to the vital facts, making them believe Germany was the wilful aggressor and that France was merely waging a war of self-defense.

10. His deceit in the letter to King George July 31, 1914, assuring him of his pacific purposes after having caused the launching of the war by the Russians.

It would be a grave mistake to permit a discussion of this great question to degenerate into stigmatizing leaders, however much they erred. Let us give Poincaré credit for believing that he was another Napoleon, leading France to a "glorious victory", to an era of "greater splendor", to the hegemony of Europe, and that his motives were inspired by patriotism. He played his part. He failed to realize the relentless law of gravity, which at last controls all human affairs. It is not yet too late for him and his group to make some amends by giving their energies to making future peace secure on a basis of open diplomacy, true democracy, justice and conciliation, and by ending the old doctrine of intrigue and violence.

IV. MOBILIZATION

General mobilization was precisely equal to a declaration of war, and was so understood throughout Europe. It involved in Russia, for example, calling to the colors fourteen million men, and a vast machinery providing instant daily supplies of food, clothing, transportation, arms and ammunition to these millions of combatants.

It meant putting the entire country under military control, and submerging the civil authorities.

It was the final act after diplomacy had utterly failed, and when nothing remained except military force. It was the roar of the cannon's mouth instead of the courteous voice of the diplomat.

General Boisdeffre, when negotiating the Franco-Russian agreement of 1892, said: "Mobilization is a declaration of war. Mobilization compels one's neighbor to do the same; mobilization involves the execution of strategic transport and of concentration," to which the Czar of Russia replied: "It is thus that I understand it." [1]

Even the strongly pro-French eminent historian, Renouvin, admits this, and says that Russian mobilization could not but provoke a reply from Germany, that is, German mobilization and war.

The eminent French publicist, M. Mathias Morhardt, in his book "Les Preuves," 291, says:

"All the governments of Europe knew that 'general mobilization meant war.' The Russian general mobilization constituted, on the highest authority, an act of aggression."

"We have on this point the cumulative testimony of Czar Alexander III; of Czar Nicholas II; of King George V; of William II, and

[1] French Yellow Book, No. 71.

M. Raymond Poincaré, and we have also the declarations of General Boisdeffre, General Obrontcheff, of General Dobrorolski, of M. Maurice Paléologue, of M. René Viviani, of Sir Edward Grey, of Lloyd George, etc., etc."

M. Morhardt says, in speaking of Germany, that:

"Threatened in her security and even in her existence by the Russian general mobilization, Germany first demanded that Russia suspend her mobilization, as proclaimed by Nicholas II in his declaration, and it was because Russia refused * * * that war became inevitable."

This verdict is supported by the ablest historians in the world—among them many distinguished Frenchmen.[1]

It is perfectly obvious from the records that the conspiracy of the Russian Imperialists and of Raymond Poincaré not only willed the war, deliberately prepared for it, created the pretext through Serbia, and falsely put the blame on the German leaders for willing the war, but then took the aggressive step of the general mobilization of Russia which began on July 24 with the order given by the ministerial counsel for mobilization, which the military clique immediately converted into a general mobilization. The Czar signed the first formal ukase ordering general mobilization July 29th, withheld it and reissued it July 30th.

On July 24th, 1914 the French Ambassador to Russia gave a luncheon attended by the Russian Minister of Foreign Affairs. This was immediately following the advice from Serbia of the Austrian ultimatum.

[1] See Supplement.

Immediately following at three o'clock a Ministerial Council was held at which the consent of the Czar was requested to order the mobilization of the Russian armies and the Russian fleets, to authorize the gathering of war materials, to authorize the withdrawal of funds from Germany and Austria. These resolutions were confirmed by the Czar July 25th, a crown council endorsed it July 25th, and all necessary measures preparatory for war were to be taken. The English Ambassador Buchanan notified his Government that the Russian Emperor had sanctioned the drafting of the Imperial Ukase which was to be published when the Minister of Foreign Affairs considered the moment had come for giving effect to it, ordering the mobilization of eleven hundred thousand men. The necessary preliminary preparations for mobilization would however be begun at once. This was July 25th.

Ambassador Buchanan further advised his Government that Sazonoff was given courage in his aggressive plans by absolute French assurance of military aid. That the French Ambassador had given Sazonoff formal assurance that France placed herself unreservedly on Russia's side. (July 25th.) So Edward Grey knew these vital facts.

General Dobrorolski, chief of mobilization of the Russian general staff, states that the Ministerial Council and general staff meeting on July 25th decided definitely upon war. This was before the Russians had learned the terms of the Serbian reply to Austria.

Dobrorolski said:

"On the evening of July 25th, 1914 a meeting of the committee of the general staff took place at which it was decided to declare at once a preparatory mobilization period and further to declare a state of war over all fortresses and frontier stations. War was already decided on. The whole flood of telegrams between the governments of Russia and Germany was merely the stage dressing behind which a drama was prepared."

He states that on the night of July the 25th a second order was dispatched:

"To reckon the 26th of July as the beginning of the period of war preparations in the whole territory of European Russia."

From that time onward the entire Russian army was as a matter of fact in a state of mobilization although the Ukase was not yet published. Dobrorolski says a partial mobilization was impossible and that he resisted any orders to that effect.

The Peace negotiations by the Russians was solely a ruse without sincerity and with no true desire for peace.

General Palizyn in the summer of 1915, at that time chief of the Russian general staff, speaking of Austria, said:

"But for a long time they did not believe that we would declare war. They devoted all their attention to Serbia in the full conviction that we would not stir. Our mobilization struck them like a thunder bolt. It was then too late for them. They had become involved with Serbia. The Germans too permitted the first days to elapse without action. Altogether we gained twelve days. Our enemies committed a huge blunder [by regarding Russian diplomacy as sincere] and conceded to us at the same time an incalculable advantage."

Premier Pashitch of Serbia wrote his chief of staff July 31, 1914 and said:

"The report received from our minister in St. Petersburg states that Russia is now negotiating and is prolonging the negotiations in order to gain time for the mobilization and concentration of her army. When her mobilization is finished she will declare war on Austria."

On July 28th Paléologue again informed Sazonoff of the complete willingness of France to fight with Russia. Sazonoff knew from dispatches from London that Germany could not rely on British neutrality and that the British Government was fully committed to France—Russia's ally—so Sazonoff pointed out to the chief of the general staff "the necessity of no further hesitation with the mobilization of the army" and on July 28th orders for a complete mobilization were made ready for the Czar's signature. He signed it July 29th and after the telegram was ready for delivery countermanded it by telephone, because of the urgent telegram from Wilhelm the Second telling him that if he ordered mobilization he would be responsible for the war which would follow. The chief of staff on July 29th telegraphed to Warsaw that "July 30th would be the first day of mobilization."

On July 29th at 3 P.M. the Russian chief of general staff falsely declared to the German military attaché at St. Petersburg upon his word of honor that up to that hour mobilization had occurred nowhere and that the Czar wished no mobilization against Germany. The Czar had already signed the Ukase.

On July 28th Sazonoff telegraphed the Russian Ambassador at Berlin that on July 29th the mobilization of four districts against Austria would be published but no aggressive purposes against Germany were entertained. This was an official falsehood. On July 24th between 11 and 12 o'clock A.M. General Janushkivich, Chief of the general staff called Dobrorolski, mobilization chief, and asked him "have you everything ready for proclaiming the mobilization of the army?" An affirmative answer was given and he was told to bring the necessary documents within an hour and that only a partial mobilization would be given out for the reason that "in carrying out such a mobilization nothing should give Germany occasion to see in it anything hostile to herself." (See Sec. 25 and 29 supplement). The preparations for war thus begun on the 24th of July and the partial mobilization so-called were in effect the immediate steps looking to general mobilization which was determined upon almost immediately and carried out without having been delayed to much greater material extent than if the general mobilization had gone into effect by being posted from the beginning. These records demonstrate beyond a doubt the warlike intention of Russia and that the French leaders were equally determined on war.

Sazonoff reporting on his mission to Paris and London in 1912 said: "Grey voluntarily confirmed to me what I already

knew from Poincaré; the existence of an arrangement between France and England, by virtue of which, in case of war
with Germany, England has incurred the obligation of lend-
ing to France her assistance, not only on sea, but also on land,
by means of landing troops on the continent."

See Ewart, p. 531.

France, with England behind her, made the Russians bold
to carry out the Russian Imperial Conspiracy to destroy
Austria and crush Germany.

In a recent Paris publication of 400 pages by sixteen
former leading generals and admirals of Nicholas II. foreword by Victor Marqueritte, entitled "Documents Historiques
des Alliées contra la Russie" the evidence against the French
leaders is set forth from a Russian view-point, but it also
convicts the Czar's government. These witnesses contend
that the French leaders intrigued Russia into the War.

By four o'clock of Thursday, the 30th of July, the Czar
had twice ordered general mobilization, which meant war and
nothing else than war against Germany under the predetermined plot of the conspirators, Sazonoff, Isvolski and Poincaré. Day by day dispatches were coming from the French
Government that France would stand firmly by Russia, and
on the night of July 31 the famous Dispatch 216 advised
Sazonoff that the French Government was determined on
war, and that the Russians should concentrate their forces
on Germany, treating Austria as a negligible quantity.

Russia took this advice, and threw 800,000 troops into East
Prussia before the Germans could rally to its defense. It was

not until midnight Friday, July 31, that Wilhelm II demanded the cessation of the Russian mobilization. When this demand was refused, the German Government did not declare war on Russia, but accepted the challenge of a state of war against Germany by Russia.

Immediately Germany was charged with having declared and started the war, and thereby held morally responsible for everything that followed, by all those who innocently accepted this artfully contrived fiction.

The moral responsibility was on Sazonoff, Nicholas II, Grand Duke Nicholas and Raymond Poincaré. Their guilt is now thoroughly established, and no well informed man has any right whatever to deny it. The evidence is complete, and has been printed by the highest authorities in many languages. (See Supplement.)

FALSIFICATIONS RUSSIAN ORANGE BOOK

V. THE FATEFUL TELEGRAMS OF JULY 1914

Telegram 184,[1] the Russian Minister of Foreign Affairs Sazonoff, on July 24, states:

"Germany ardently desired the localization of the conflict, as the interference of any other power on the ground of existing treaties must have incalculable consequences. * * * Ex-Minister Pichon had an interview with the Austrian Ambassador today, from which he also gained the impression that *Austria-Hungary did not intend her step to be regarded as an unconditional ultimatum."*

[1] Falsification of the Russian Orange Book, p. 21.

Telegram 186, from the Russian representative at Paris to Sazonoff, Petrograd, on July 25, said that the action of the German Ambassador—

"Has to some extent reassured the foreign ministry as being an indication that *Germany does not seek for war in any case.*" * * *

That the German Ambassador had pointed out—

"That the Austrian note has not the character of an ultimatum"; * * * "that the *German step had only for its object the localization of the Austro-Serbian conflict;* * * * that the absence of the President of the Republic and of the Minister President (Viviani) *prevents the foreign office for the moment from expressing its opinion definitely regarding present events."*

Telegram 187, July 26, from the Russian representative at Paris to Sazonoff, Petrograd, states that the German Ambassador had advised the French Minister for Foreign Affairs:

"Austria has declared to Russia that she seeks no territorial gains and does not threaten the integrity of Serbia. Her sole object is to secure her own peace and to maintain order."

Telegram 188, July 26, from the Paris Russian representative to Sazonoff, says that Berthelot, the director of the political department of France, inclines to the opinion—

"That Germany and Austria do not desire war in any case."

These Russian telegrams from their highest authorities are evidence of commanding importance showing the earnest desire of the Germans and Austrians to localize and adjust the conflict and to avoid a general European war. The Russians would not permit it.

Telegram 1521, July 27, Sazonoff, Russian Foreign Minister, to Isvolski, Russian Ambassador in Paris:

"If there is a question of exercising a moderating influence in Petersburg, we reject it in advance, as we have adopted a standpoint from the outset which we can in no way alter." * * *

The *Russian Standpoint* is clearly set forth in the Treaty of 1892-1894; the Franco-Russian military conferences and the Crown Councils favoring a general war.

Telegram 194, Isvolski wired that Poincaré will return to Paris on Wednesday, July 29 (five days after Belgian mobilization, four days after Russian preparatory mobilization had begun) and two nights later, July 31, the French Minister of War told the Russian Military Attaché the French Government was determined on war, (telegram 216).

Telegram 195, July 27th, the German Ambassador is shown urging a new proposal for the intervention of France and Germany between Russia and Austria, which was not accepted. Isvolski says in this regard:

"I was surprised at the *correct* understanding of the situation manifested by the acting minister and his assistant and to see *how firm and tranquil they were in their determination to extend to us their fullest support* and to avoid the slightest appearance of any lack of unity between us."

Telegram 197, July 27, Isvolski to Sazonoff:

"M. Cambon (French Ambassador in Berlin) telegraphs from Berlin that in reply to his questions as *to what attitude Germany would adopt toward a partial mobilization by Russia,* Jagow (German secretary of state for foreign affairs) replied that a *mobilization of that kind* would not result in German mobilization, but *that if Russia attacked Austria, Germany would immediately reply by attacking Russia.*"

Telegram 1539, July 28, Sazonoff to Isvolski:

"In consequence of Austro-Hungary's declaration of war against Serbia, we shall announce tomorrow a mobilization of the Odessa, Kieff, Moscow and Kazan military districts. *In bringing this to the notice of the German Government repeat that Russia has no aggressive intentions against Germany. Meanwhile* our Ambassador in Vienna is not being recalled."

Sazonoff directed his Ambassador to state a falsehood to the German Government. Russia did have aggressive intentions against Germany. The testimony of Dobrorolski, Sukhomlinoff, Isvolski, Palinzy, Pashitch, and Sazonoff himself prove it.

Sukhomlinoff had already issued a general mobilization order of the Russian Army. He "lied to the Czar" as to its being a general mobilization,[1] said it was *partial,* and pretended that he had stopped the mobilization, although he did not do so. The Czar however, July 30, authorized the general mobilization.[2]

Telegram 198, July 28, Isvolski to Sazonoff:

"I deem it my duty to make clear that, as results from my conversation yesterday at the Quai d'Orsay, the acting *French Minister for Foreign Affairs did not for a moment admit the possibility of*

[1] "Eggerling."
[2] Let France Explain, p. 201.

exercising a moderating influence in Petersburg. * * * As a result of his conversation with Baron Schön, the Minister declined to accept the German proposal."

The French Foreign Minister was not willing to work for peace. One resolute telegram to Russia demanding peace would have sufficed.

Germany was strenuously exercising a moderating influence on Vienna in favor of peace.

On July 30 the German Chancellor telegraphed the German Ambassador at Vienna to notify Austria that Germany *"must refuse* to be drawn into a world conflagration *frivolously and in disregard of our advice.*

Telegram 201, July 28, Isvolski to Sazonoff, states that the German Ambassador had again visited the French Foreign Minister and told him that:

"Germany solely desired to work with France for the maintenance of peace. * * * *That Germany was ready to co-operate with the* other powers for the maintenance of peace."

Telegram 1544, Sazonoff to Isvolski, July 29:

"The German Ambassador informed me on behalf of the Imperial Chancellor that Germany had not ceased and *will not cease to exercise a moderating influence in Vienna, and would continue to do so despite the declaration of war.* Up to this morning no news has been received of the crossing of Austrian troops on to Serbian territory."

Telegram 1551, July 29, Sazonoff to Isvolski:

"The German Ambassador has communicated to me today the decision of his government to mobilize *if Russia does not stop her military preparation.* * * * As we can not accede to Germany's wish, nothing remains for us but *to hasten our own warlike preparations and to reckon with the probable inevitability of war. Inform the French Government of this, and at the same time thank it for its declaration made in its name by the French Ambassador that we can fully rely upon the support of our ally, France.* Under present circumstances this declaration is especially valuable for us. It is *very desirable that England also without loss of time should associate herself with France and Russia, as it is only thus that she can succeed in preventing a dangerous alteration in the European balance.* London telegraphed to in like terms."

The war contract was in action. The association of Great Britain with Russia and France would guarantee the safety of attack by Russia on Germany.

Telegram 304, July 29, Sazonoff to Isvolski:

"I *urgently* request you to communicate to the French Foreign Minister the following telegram from the French Ambassador in Petersburg: *"The German Ambassador has just informed Sazonoff that if Russia does not stop her military preparations the German Army will be ordered to mobilize."* * * *

Telegram 202, July 29, Isvolski to Sazonoff:

"Bienvenu-Martin, the acting Foreign Minister, told me that this morning the *German Ambassador made a communication* to him, employing practically the following expressions: *"Germany is continuing her endeavors in Vienna to cause Austria to agree to a friendly exchange of opinions* which should indicate the object and the extent of the steps undertaken by her and concerning which Germany has not so far been exactly informed. The declaration of war will not stand in the way of this exchange of opinions. *Germany hopes to receive during the course of these negotiations explanations which will satisfy Russia.* Finally, Baron Schön again protested against the assertion that Germany was encouraging Austria to be unyielding."

Telegram 203, July 29, Isvolski to Sazonoff:

* * * *"Germany* * * * declares that as we have received the assurance that Austria seeks no territorial gains, the maintenance of peace entirely depends on Russia* because it turns upon the necessity for localizing the Austro-Serbian affair; that is, the punishment of Serbia for her former policy and the giving of guarantees for the future." * * *

He states:

"That France and England positively could not exercise any moderating influence in Russia." * * *

A single telegram from Poincaré to the Czar refusing to approve a general war would have prevented the World War. A vigorous demand from Edward Grey on Poincaré and Sazonoff might have prevented the War.

The World War was already on under the secret contract, and that very night, July 29, Poincaré, Viviani and the Minister of War at a confidential meeting agreed to stand firmly for war. (Barnes). On this very day the Czar ordered a general mobilization—the Russian equivalent of war—suspended it and reordered it the next day, Thursday, July 30. The British fleet was fully mobilized and so were Serbia and Belgium.

Telegram 204, July 29, Wednesday, Isvolski to Sazonoff:

"The firm attitude taken up by the French press continues. It passes severe judgment upon the Austrian attack and *upon Germany's manifest share of blame for it, and unhesitatingly declares that this touches us,* and *that we can not remain unsympathetic. As regards solidarity with us,* this question is not once discussed, but is taken as

a matter of course. *Every journalist expresses himself in* this sense, including such prominent personages belonging to the most diverse parties as Pichon, Clemenceau, and even Jaurés, and also Hervé, the father of antimilitarism."

The press reflected the French Government's wishes. *A part had been subsidized with Russian money, a part was moved by nationalism and the certainty of victory.*

Telegram 206, July 29, Isvolski to Sazonoff:

"When the President returned to Paris, he was received at the railway station and in the streets with sympathetic demonstrations from the assembled crowd. Margerie (political director in the French Foreign Office) told me that the President, from his conversations with prefects and politicians during his journey, had become convinced of the *firm, energetic,* and at the same time *calm state of public opinion, which plainly formed a correct estimate of the true significance of events.* The same attitude reigned among a large section of the Radical Socialists. The government attaches no importance to the antimilitary demonstrations of the revolutionary party, and intends to take energetic measures against it. *Our military attaché reports in detail regarding the preparatory military measures. Feeling runs high in military circles and in the chief command.* I report regarding the press in a special telegram."

Telegram 207, July 29, Isvolski to Sazonoff, shows further efforts on the part of Germany to get an adjustment and states:

"Finally Baron Schön complained of France's military preparations, and said that in this case *Germany would be compelled* to adopt similar precautions. Viviani, on his part, declared that France honestly desired peace, but at the same time *was firmly determined to act in full agreement with her allies,* and *Baron Schön could con-*

vince himself that this decision was finding the liveliest support in the country. This evening Viviani has forbidden a projected anti-war meeting of the revolutionary party."

On the night of July 31st the French Minister of War told the military attache that the French Government was determined on war.

Telegram 1554, Sazonoff to Isvolski, states that if Austria would admit that the Austro-Serbian question had assumed the character of a European question and would declare a readiness to eliminate from her ultimatum those points which violate the sovereign rights of Serbia, *Russia would undertake to suspend her military preparations.*

These preparations had been going on for at least five days. The Russian policy was to use diplomatic negotiations to conceal the war measures, and the Russian policy fixed in 1912 was to cross the German border without a declaration of war.[1]

Telegram 1555, July 30, Sazonoff wires Isvolski:

"Until we receive a *thoroughly* satisfactory reply from Austria through the German Government, *we shall continue our military preparations.* This is communicated to you very confidentially."

The word "thoroughly" is interesting. It suggests that Austria's reply, whatever it might be, would not be satisfactory.

That very night (July 31), at 1 A. M., August 1, Isvolski telegraphed to Sazonoff, telegram 216:

[1] Von Kuhl, p. 79-80.

"*From military attache to War Minister, 1 A. M.*

The French War Minister informed me in earnest, hearty tones (sincerite enthusiastique) *that the Government is firmly decided upon war, and requested me to confirm the hope of the French general staff that all our efforts will be directed against Germany, and that Austria will be treated as a quantite negligible.*"

This was a secret French and Russian official declaration of war even if not following the usual forms. The Czar had already on the 30th of July renewed the order for a general Russian mobilization, the Russian equivalent of war.

This attitude was strictly in line with the Franco-Russian secret treaty of 1892 and the military plans worked out by the French and Russian general staffs in annual conferences and frequent intercommunications.

So that the French Government gave Austria no time to make "a *thoroughly* satisfactory" reply to Russia or any other kind of reply, and indicates that Sazonoff wanted none.

On August 1, telegram 1601, Sazonoff wired Isvolski:

"At midnight the German Ambassador informed me on behalf of his government *that if within twelve hours*—that is, before midday on Saturday—*we do not begin to demobilize, not only as against Germany, but also as against Austria, the German Government will be compelled to order mobilization.* To my query as to *whether this was equivalent to a declaration of war,* the Ambassador replied that *it was not,* but added that *we were very near to war.*"

On Saturday, August 1, at 5 P. M., Germany issued a general order of mobilization; at 7.10 P. M. the German Ambassador notified Sazonoff that Germany accepted the war challenge of Russia. The negotiation with Austria and Germany for the *preservation of peace appears to have been used as a camouflage for a predetermined war.*

Telegram 208, July 30, from Isvolski to Sazonoff, assured him:

"The French Government is ready to fulfill all its obligations as an ally. It is of opinion, however, that at the present moment, when negotiations are still in progress between the less interested powers, it would be to the purpose that Russia, so far as the measures of a defensive and precautionary nature which it has deemed necessary to adopt will permit, should not take any direct step which would serve Germany as a pretext for ordering the general or partial mobilization of her forces."

This dispatch was based on the authority of a decision made by Poincaré, Viviani and Messimy.

"Defensive" meant *"offensive"* by General Staff interpretation and this telegram meant—we are ready; press your war measures and keep Germany in the dark.

The significance of this suppressed telegram is revealed in combination with telegram 1551 of July 29 and suppressed telegrams 209 and 210 and 216 from Paris on July 30.

The French Government having determined on war, did not wish Germany to mobilize yet, but gradually to discover a situation so dangerous that she must declare a state of war existing as a military necessity. Then the Russian and French leaders could and did fix the blame on Germany for breach of the peace. This was brilliantly done.

Telegram 1551, on July 29, from Sazonoff to Isvolski, stated:

"Nothing remains for us but to hasten our own warlike preparations and to reckon with the probable *inevitability of war. Inform the French Government of this* and *at the same time thank it for its declaration * * * that we can fully rely upon the support of our ally, France."*

This was two days before the German Government demanded that the Russian mobilization should stop under a penalty of German mobilization and three days before the German Ambassador at Petersburg accepted a state of war as forced on the German Government. It was not a German declaration of war. It was a German acceptance of a state of war organized and made against Germany on a pretext that was frivolous and false. Neither Russian, French nor British interests were menaced by Austria or Germany.

Telegram 209, of July 30, Isvolski to Sazonoff, states that the French Ambassador in London:

"Was instructed to confer with Grey as to the fixing of the combined attitude of France and England concerning which these two powers, in *consequence of the general understanding existing between them,* have *to deliberate* whenever a period of political tension arises."

The time "to deliberate" had nearly arrived.

This proposed conference was based on the notes exchanged between Cambon and Grey on the 22nd and 23rd of November, 1912,[1] and the war plans of the military and naval staffs of Great Britain, France and Russia, already completely matured.

Telegram 210, of July 30, from Isvolski to Sazonoff, said

[1] Exhibits 8 and 9, How Diplomats Make War.

that *the French War Minister had said to the Russian military attaché:*

> * * * *"that we could declare that in the higher interests of peace we are ready temporarily to delay our preparations for mobilization, since this would not prevent us from continuing our preparations and indeed from intensifying them, but we should have to refrain as far as possible from transporting troops in masses."*

These suppressed telegrams indicate that both in Petersburg and in Paris the negotiations for the maintenance of peace were "a ruse de guerre" and being used as a screen for a war already fully determined on both in Paris and in Petersburg.

Telegram 216, of July 31, Isvolski to Sazonoff, expressed a fixed war determination.

On the same day, July 31, telegram from Isvolski to Sazonoff discloses that Baron Schön asked Viviani what attitude France would adopt in the event of an armed collision between Russia and Germany. *Viviani declined to answer.* Baron Schön requested arrangements for passports.

On August 1 the German Ambassador again visited Viviani, and the latter expressed his "astonishment" to Baron Schön at his action yesterday, "which was not justified by the relations between France and Germany," although, as above, the French Government had already decided upon war and advised Russia to attack Germany with all its forces—and Viviani knew it as premier.

Isvolski to Sazonoff, August 1, telegram 219, states that

the German Ambassador had visited Viviani for the second time. That Viviani informed him that the President of the Republic, *Poincaré, had signed a decree ordering French mobilization.* (It may be remembered that the formal public order of Belgian mobilization was issued July 31 also, although the army had been mobilized on and before July 24.) Viviani expressed his astonishment that Germany should have adopted such a measure as demanding that Russia demobilize under penalty of a German mobilization—

"when a friendly exchange of views was in progress between Russia, Austria and the other powers."

Here is the refinement of high-class diplomacy. Two nations have fully prepared themselves for war, are determined on war against a neighbor, and yet the Premier of France assures the Ambassador of Germany that a friendly exchange of views between the powers forbids Germany to prepare for defense!

And the same day, August 1, Isvolski wires Sazonoff:

"Poincaré declared to me in the most categorical manner that both he himself and the whole cabinet are firmly determined fully to carry out the obligations laid upon us by the terms of our alliance."

That meant that Russia could go to war with confidence, that France was ready and would carry out the secret contract and attack Germany simultaneously.

The French general mobilization and an immediate offensive on Germany were required by the secret Russian agreement of 1892.

Isvolski, Russian Ambassador, wired Sazonoff the same day, August 1, 1914, telegram 223, as follows:

"Poincaré told me that during the last few days the Austrian Ambassador had energetically assured him and Viviani that Austria had declared to us (Russia) her readiness not only to respect the territorial integrity of Serbia but also her sovereign rights, but that we (Russia) had intentionally concealed those assurances. To my remark that this was a complete lie, Poincaré replied that similar statements had been made in London by Austria, where they might create a very dangerous impression, and therefore ought to be denied there as well."

That Austria did make these representations is shown by telegram 195; by a verbal declaration of Count Pourtales, German Ambassador in St. Petersburg; and by Sazonoff's answer contained in the first two sentences from St. Petersburg of telegram 1554, and by many other records.

The attitude of Italy is shown by telegram 220 of August 1, from Isvolski to Sazonoff, as follows:

"Margerie told me that according to information from a *very secret source* Italy apparently intends, in reliance upon the manner in which the conflict has arisen, *to remain neutral at first, and then to come to one decision or another in accordance with the course of events."*

The Entente had already weakened Italy's attachment to Germany by concessions in Africa and elsewhere.

Von Moltke's memorandum of 1912 as the chief of the German general staff, showed that the Germans did not count upon Italy.[1]   That Germany could not compete on the ocean with Britain or on land with Russia; that Germany had but little hope in a war with Russia and France.

Austria accepted the proposed mediation as between herself and Serbia as two sovereign governments,[2] but it availed nothing.

Petrograd knew of Austria's acceptance of mediation which was disclosed to Grey in London on the 1st of August.[3]

Sazonoff, former Russian Minister of Foreign Affairs, seven years later, November 15, 1921, in *La Revue de France,* tells that the Czar received a telegram from the Kaiser begging the Czar, notwithstanding the declaration of war, to keep the troops from the German frontier, and *that the German Emperor was nearly frantic.*

Baron Rosen in "Forty Years of Diplomatic Life", Saturday Evening Post, August 21, 1920, page 85, gives it as his opinion *that the Russian mobilization necessarily led to war.* He places the guilt upon all three Russian heads, *Sazonoff, Sukhomlinoff, and Jaunuschkevitch.* He states that at dinner with Sukhomlinoff, then Minister of War, when he received a telegram that Austria-Hungary had mobilized against Serbia (July 25), he heard the war minister exclaim—

[1] Congressional Record, 392.
[2] Austrian Red Book III, p. 65.
[3] British White Book, 133.

"Cette Fois Nous Marcherons!"

that is, "This time we shall march."[1] This meant under the treaty, 1892, the military and naval conventions with France that Russia would attack Germany.

France would follow, as by treaty required, and England would instantly support France as Edward Grey "voluntarily" told Sazonoff when visiting Grey in 1912.

Baron Rosen states that *the intelligencia and military party of Russia were for war.*[2] They controlled the government.

Baron Rosen further tells that Sazonoff and Jaunuschkevitch stopped the dispatch of the Czar's aide to Berlin and secured on Thursday, July 30, *a re-order of the general mobilization.*[3]

It was in this condition of affairs, with Russia having an army of over 2,000,000 men on the east, who had been practicing mobilization since spring and actually had been in process of mobilizing at least since the 25th of July (Czar's telegram), that the German Government demanded the mobilization stopped under the alleged necessity of regarding it as a declaration of war by Russia.

It was well understood by the military strategists of France and Russia and of Europe that Germany's only chance in such a war as this was by lightning speed and efficiency, striking France through Belgium.   (See French and Rus-

[1] Rosen, July 24, 1920, 132.
[2] Rosen, August 21, 1920.
[3] Rosen, August 21, 1920.

sian military conferences.)   The dispatches show that Germany tried to secure French neutrality and failed, tried to obtain British neutrality and failed, tried to induce Belgium to submit to an unopposed passage and failed.[1]

VI. THE RUSSIAN GOAL

In Stieve's book "Isvolski and the World War", page 187, will be found an analysis of Sazonoff's report of December 8, 1913, which shows that the previous attempt of Russia to control the Dardanelles, through the breaking up of Turkey, was impracticable because of the opposition of France, which had great financial resources invested in Turkey.   In this report the following language reveals the policy of Sazonoff:

"Moreover, I must repeat that the question of the Straits can hardly be advanced a step except through European complications. To judge from present conditions, these complications would find us in alliance with France and possibly, but not quite certainly, with Great Britain, or at least with the latter as a benevolent neutral. In the event of European complications, we should be able to count in the Balkans on Serbia and perhaps also on Roumania.   This makes clear the task of our diplomacy, which consists of creating favorable conditions for as close a rapprochement with Roumania as possible. This policy must be pursued uninterruptedly, cautiously and open-mindedly." * * *

This report met the Czar's approval.

On February 8, 1914, there met, this time with Sazonoff

[1] Morel, Truth and the War.   How Diplomats Make War, Neilson. Diplomatic Documents, World War, Scott.

himself in the chair, a fresh conference with the heads of the Russian Army and Navy, in which preparations for conquest of the Straits were discussed on the basis of the report to the Czar of December 8, 1913. The minutes contained the following record:

> *"Replying to the question whether * * * we could count on support from Serbia, S. D. Sazonoff said that it could not be assumed that our operations against the Straits could take place without a general European war, and that it was assumed that under such circumstances Serbia would direct all her forces against Austria-Hungary.*
>
> *"With reference to what the Foreign Minister had said concerning the general situation in which a decision of the question of the Straits might be expected, the chief of the general staff expressed his conviction that the struggle for Constantinople would hardly be possible without a general European war."* [1]

All the ministers were advised to adopt all measures required to facilitate the plans of the contemplated war.

So the military leaders supported Sazonoff.

The Czar himself entered on the minutes of the conference the following:

"I entirely approve the decisions of the conference."

This and the fuller record referred to clearly show that the plan laid in 1892 and in the French and Russian military conferences was being still carried out, and that its object was to control the Dardanelles, exercise Balkan hegemony, and the means was a general European war, with Serbia, Rou-

[1] Stieve, p. 230.

mania, France, Great Britain and Japan as allies. And so it happened.

It was in February, 1914, that the Czar assured the Serbian minister of his support in the war and in which the Serbian minister asked for 120,000 rifles and said his country would supply 500,000 men. For months before the war Russian war supplies were pouring into Serbia.

On July 24 the Czar approved a pretended partial mobilization. On July 29 the Czar approved a general mobilization order, and reordered on July 30 the general mobilization of all of Russia's forces, involving 14,000,000 men. It meant nothing less than war.

CHAPTER V

GERMANY, AUSTRIA, BELGIUM AND ENGLAND IN 1914

I. Some Evidence From Berlin

It was the policy of Germany to support Austria in re-buking Serbia, as far as could be done through diplomacy, but even if the diplomatic effort should fail, Germany did not intend to be drawn into a war.

On Sunday, the 26th of July, the Kaiser returned from his Scandinavian cruise. On Monday a rapid fire of tele-grams took place from Berlin to Vienna, under the instructions of the Kaiser, demanding a peaceful adjustment, Berlin assuming that the purpose of the Entente was not necessarily hostile or determined on war, and that the negotiations for a peaceful settlement were really sincere, put great pressure on the Austrian Government, as appears, through the following telegrams:

From the German Chancellor to the German Ambassador, Vienna,
July 27:

"We can not reject the rôle of mediator and must place the English proposal before the Vienna cabinet for consideration. Request

Count Berchtold's opinion on the British proposal, as well as on Sazonoff's wish to negotiate directly with Vienna." [1]

On July 28 the Chancellor sent this dispatch:

"The refusal of every exchange of views with Petrograd would be a serious mistake if it provokes Russia precisely to armed interference, which Austria is primarily interested in avoiding. We are ready, to be sure, to fulfill our obligations as an ally, but *must refuse to allow ourselves to be drawn by Vienna into a world conflagration frivolously* and *in disregard of our advice.* Please say this to Count Berchtold *at once with all emphasis and with great seriousness.*" [2]

On July 28 Austria declared war against Serbia in order to escape from the German pressure to avoid even a local war which Wilhelm II thought no longer necessary. Austria was determined to punish Serbia, but did not want a general war.

On July 29 the German Chancellor sent this dispatch:

"I regard the attitude of the Austrian Government and its unparalleled procedure toward the various governments with increasing astonishment. * * * It leaves us wholly in the dark as to its program. * * * I must conclude that the Austrian Government is harboring plans which it sees fit to conceal from us in order to assure herself in all events of German support and avoid the refusal which might result from a frank statement." [3]

He sent five warning telegrams on the 29th and 30th to Vienna. [4]

The Kaiser had informed Foreign Minister Jagow on see-

[1] Die Deutschen Dokumente, No. 396.
[2] Ibid., No. 396.
[3] Die Deutschen Dokumente, No. 396, p. 361.
[4] Ibid.

ing the Serbian reply accepting most of the Austrian conditions and agreeing to mediation that—

"Now, no cause for war any longer exists."

On July 30 the German Chancellor sent the following telegram:

"If Austria refuses all negotiations, we are face to face with a conflagration *in which England will be against us. Roumania and Italy,* according to all indications, *will not be for us,* and we shall stand *two against four powers.* Through England's opposition the main blow will fall on Germany. Austria's political prestige, the military honor of her army, as well as her just claims against Serbia, can be adequately satisfied by her occupation of Belgrade or other places. Through her humiliation of Serbia she will make her position in the Balkans, as well as her relation to Russia, strong again. Under these circumstances, *we must urgently and emphatically press* upon the consideration of the Vienna Cabinet the *adoption of mediation* in accordance with the above honorable conditions. The responsibility for the consequences which would otherwise follow would be for Austria and for us an uncommonly heavy one." [1]

On July 31st Austria finally made the concessions required but they were of no consequence as the World War was already in full swing, as the conspirators intended.

The Austrian statesmen intended only a local war to obtain guarantees of peace from Serbia and were willing to mediate, but the Russian statesmen who had instigated the deeds leading to the local war used it as a pretext for the World War, the French leaders cooperating.

In Oman's Outbreak of the War, pages 61, 68, 69, 77, 79,

[1] German White Book, p. 395.

88 and 89, will be found the exchange of telegrams between William II and Nicholas, as follows:

(Tuesday) July 28—10.45 P. M.

"I have heard with the greatest anxiety of the impression which is caused by the action of Austria-Hungary against Serbia. The unscrupulous agitation which had been going on for years in Serbia has led to the revolting crime of which Archduke Franz Ferdinand has become a victim. The spirit which made the Serbians murder their own King and his consort still dominates that country. Doubtless you will agree with me that both of us, you as well as I, and all other sovereigns, have a common interest to insist that all those who are responsible for this horrible murder shall suffer their deserved punishment.

On the other hand, I by no means overlook the difficulty encountered by you and your government to stem the tide of public opinion. In view of the cordial friendship which has joined us both for a long time with firm ties, *I shall use my entire influence to induce Austria-Hungary to obtain a frank and satisfactory understanding with Russia. I hope confidently that you will support me in my efforts to overcome all difficulties which may yet arise.*

Your most sincere and devoted friend and cousin,

WILHELM." [1]

Peterhof Palace, July 29—1 P. M.

"I am glad that you are back in Germany. In this serious moment I ask you earnestly to help me. An ignominious war has been declared against a weak country, and in Russia the indignation, which I fully share, is tremendous. I fear that very soon *I shall be unable to resist the pressure exercised upon me, and that I shall be forced to take measures which will lead to war.*

To prevent such a calamity as a European war would be, I urge you

[1] Oman's Outbreak of the War, p. 61.

in the name of our old friendship to do all in your power to restrain your ally from going too far."

NICHOLAS.[1]

Russian war preparations had been in progress five days, and on July 29 and again on the 30th of July, Nicholas ordered the general mobilization of all of Russia's forces—the Russian equivalent of war.

(Wednesday) July 29—6.30 P. M.

"I have received your telegram and I share your desire for the conservation of peace. However, I can not—as I told you in my first telegram—consider the action of Austria-Hungary as an 'ignominious war.' Austria-Hungary knows from experience that the promises of Serbia, as long as they are merely on paper, are entirely unreliable. According to my opinion the action of Austria-Hungary is to be considered as an attempt to receive full guaranty that the promises of Serbia are effectively translated into deeds. In this opinion I am strengthened by the explanation of the Austrian Cabinet that Austria-Hungary intended no territorial gain at the expense of Serbia. I am therefore of opinion that it is perfectly possible for Russia to remain a spectator in the Austro-Serbian War without drawing Europe into the most terrible war it has ever seen. I believe that a direct understanding is possible and desirable between your government and Vienna, an understanding which, as I have already telegraphed you, *my government endeavors to aid with all possible effort. Naturally, military measures by Russia,* which might be construed as a menace by Austria-Hungary, *would accelerate a calamity* which both of us desire to avoid, and would undermine my position as mediator, which, upon your appeal to my friendship and aid, I willingly accepted." [2]

WILHELM.

[1] Oman's Outbreak of the War, p. 61.
[2] Ibid., p. 68.

It was the night of the 29th of July that Poincaré, Viviani and the French Minister of War decided on war.

It was two nights later that the French Minister of War said the French Government was determined on War (Telegram 216) and Isvolski so advised Sazonoff.

Peterhof Palace, July 29.

"Thanks for your telegram, which is conciliatory, while the official message presented by your Ambassador to my Foreign Minister was conveyed in a very different tone. I beg you to explain the difference. It would be right to give over the Austro-Serbia problem to The Hague Conference. I trust in your wisdom and friendship."

NICHOLAS.[1]

The alleged difference was a fiction.   (Dickinson.)

Nicholas conceals from Wilhelm that he had signed the general order for mobilizing 14,000,000 men.

Telegram to Nicholas, the Czar:

July 30—1 A. M.

"My ambassador has instructions to direct the attention of your government to the dangers and *serious consequences of a mobilization. I have told you the same in my last telegram.* Austria-Hungary has mobilized only against Serbia, and only a part of her army. If Russia, as seems to be the case, according to your advice and that of your Government, mobilizes against Austria-Hungary, the part of the mediator, with which you have intrusted me in such friendly manner and which I have accepted upon your express desire, is threatened, if not made impossible. *The entire weight of decision now rests upon your shoulders; you have to bear the responsibility of war or peace."*

WILHELM.[2]

[1] Oman's Outbreak of the War, p. 69.

[2] Ibid., p. 77

This was the day the Czar reordered Russian mobilization and at a time the French Government was determined on war. Of all which Wilhelm was kept in the dark.

Peterhof, July 30—1.20 P. M.

"I thank you from my heart for your quick reply. I am sending tonight Tatischeff (Russian honorary aid to the Kaiser) with instructions. *The military measures now taking form were decided upon five days ago,* and for the reason of defense against the preparedness of Austria. I hope with all my heart that these measures will not influence in any manner your position as mediator, which I appraise very highly. We need your strong pressure upon Austria so that an understanding can be arrived at with us."

NICHOLAS.[1]

"The military measures now taking form" was a general mobilization.

He tried to send his aide—Tatischeff, but Sazonoff seized him at the railroad station. He again ordered the general mobilization.

Poincaré, Viviani and the French Minister of War had in council the night before, July 29, firmly decided on war. Wireless telegraphy was in existence to assist speedy intercommunication.

Then Nicholas reordered Russian mobilization, involving 14,000,000 men, and wired Wilhelm. (Dobrorolski.)

Telegram to Wilhelm II from the Czar:

July 31, 1914.

"I thank you cordially for your mediation, which permits the hope that everything may yet end peaceably. *It is technically impossible to*

[1] German White Book, 1915, 23-A.

discontinue our military preparations, which have been neces-
sary by the Austrian mobilization. It is far from us to want war.
As long as the negotiations between Austria and Serbia continue, my
troops will undertake no provocative action. I give you my solemn
word thereon. I confide with all my faith in the grace of God, and
I hope for the success of your mediation in Vienna for the welfare
of our countries and the peace of Europe."

NICHOLAS.[1]

Nicholas could have stopped the mobilization. The mobilization was not due to Austria but to the secret contract of
Russia and France to attack Germany.

Under the 1892 treaty a partial Austrian mobilization required Russia and France to attack Germany. The Austrian-
Serbian negotiations could end when Nicholas said the word
and Russia was ready to enter Germany.

The negotiations were only a ruse of war.

Telegram of Wilhelm to Nicholas, Friday

July 31—2 P. M.

"Upon your appeal to my friendship and your request for my aid,
I have engaged in mediation between your government and the gov-
ernment of Austria-Hungary. While this action was taking place
your troops were being mobilized against my ally, Austria-Hungary,
whereby, as I have already communicated to you, my mediation has
become almost illusory. In spite of this I have continued it, and *I*
now receive reliable news that serious preparations for war are going
on on my eastern frontier. The responsibility for the security of my
country forces me to measures of defense. I have gone to the
extreme limit of the possible in my efforts for the preservation of the
peace of the world. It is not I who bear the responsibility for the
misfortune which now threatens the entire civilized world. It rests
in your hand to avert it. No one threatens the honor and peace of
Russia, which might well have awaited the success of my media-

[1] Oman's Outbreak of the War, p. 88.

tion. *The friendship for you and your country, bequeathed to me by my grandfather on his deathbed, has always been sacred to me, and I have stood faithfully by Russia while it was in serious affliction, especially during its last war.* The peace of Europe can still be preserved by you *if Russia decides to discontinue those military preparations* which menace Germany and Austria-Hungary."

WILHELM.[1]

No reply. Wilhelm, at midnight Friday, gave notice that the German Army would mobilize if by noon Saturday Russian mobilization did not stop. At 5 P. M. Saturday, August 1, German mobilization was issued. At 7.10 P. M., the German Ambassador at Petrograd advised the Russian Government that the Russian challenge and the state of war forced on Germany were accepted.

It will be observed in this exchange of telegrams that *Nicholas was under a pressure he feared he should be unable to resist.* On the very day that the Kaiser advised him that he would have to bear the responsibility of war or peace if he ordered a general mobilization, *he reordered the mobilization which had been begun by his own statement on July 25;* and on July 31, having the day before ordered the general mobilization, he advised the Kaiser that it was impossible to discontinue the military preparations, and he gave his solemn word that the Russian troops would undertake no provocative action, although in fact they crossed the German border in four places the next day.[2]   It is quite clear that the Czar's *solemn word* was not worthy of trust.

[1] Oman's Outbreak of the War, p. 89.
[2] Kuhl, 79-80.

The German leaders, getting daily reports from Paris, London, Brussels and Petersburg, accepted what they had become convinced was now absolutely unavoidable, and on Saturday, 5 P. M., August 1, ordered a general mobilization, and two hours later recognized the existence of the war forced on them.

The men directing the foreign affairs of Russia and France gave diplomacy no time and no chance to avoid the general War which was fully predetermined by them.

To the Germans surrounding his residence Saturday, August 1, 1914, Chancellor Bethmann Hollweg said: "The whole work of Emperor William has been devoted to the maintenance of peace. Should all his efforts prove vain and should the sword be forced into our hands we will take the field with a clear conscience in the knowledge that we did not seek war. We shall then wage war for our existence." (N. Y. TIMES.)

The German Ambassador at St. Petersburg on August 1, at 7.10 P. M., presented the following note:

"The Imperial German Government has used every effort since the beginning of the crisis to bring about a peaceful settlement. In compliance with a wish expressed to him by His Majesty the Emperor of Russia, the German Emperor had undertaken, in concert with Great Britain, the part of mediator between the cabinets of Vienna and St. Petersburg; but Russia, without waiting for any result, proceeded to a general mobilization of her forces both on land and sea. In consequence of this threatening step, which was not justified by any military proceedings on the part of Germany, the German Empire was faced by a grave and imminent danger. If the German Govern-

ment had failed to guard against this peril, they would have com-
promised the safety and the very existence of Germany. The German Government was, therefore, obliged to make representations to
the government of His Majesty the Emperor of All the Russias and
to insist upon a cessation of the aforesaid military acts. Russia having
refused to comply with (not having considered it necessary to answer)
this demand, and having shown by this refusal (this attitude) that
her action was directed against Germany, I have the honor, on the
instructions of my government, to inform Your Excellency as follows:

"His Majesty the Emperor, my august sovereign, in the name of
the German Empire, accepts the challenge and considers himself at
war with Russia."

POURTALÈS.

The words in parentheses occur in the original. It must
be supposed that two variations had been prepared in advance, and that by mistake they were both inserted in the
note.

Deutsche Documente Vol. III. p. 51.

II. KAISER WILHELM DID NOT WILL THE WAR

On July 31 William II appended the following note to the
telegram of Count Pourtalés, the German Ambassador at St.
Petersburg, advising of the Russian decision to take the
fatal step of mobilization. This memorandum by the Kaiser
shows the condition of his mind, and what he thought; shows
that he was strongly opposed to World War; shows that he
regarded it as absolutely forced upon the German people,
and shows that he intuitively diagnosed the Russian con-

spiracy against Germany; he regarded the war as ruinous to Germany and was almost frantic:

"If mobilization can no longer be retracted—*which is not true*—why, then, did the Czar appeal to my mediation three days afterward without mention of the issuance of the mobilization order? That shows plainly that the mobilization appeared to him to have been precipitate (the Kaiser was too generous; it was a ruse of war) and that after it he made this move pro forma in our direction for the sake of quieting his uneasy conscience, although he knew that it would no longer be of any use, as he did not feel himself to be strong enough to stop the mobilization. Frivolity and weakness are to plunge the world into the most frightful war, which eventually aims at the destruction of Germany. For I have no doubt left about it: *England, Russia and France have agreed among themselves —after laying the foundation of the casus foederis for us through Austria—to take the Austro-Serbian conflict for an excuse for waging a war of extermination against us.* Hence Grey's cynical observation to Lichnowsky 'as long as the war is confined to Russia and Austria, England would sit quiet,' only when we and France mixed into it would he be compelled to make an active move against us (?); i. e., either we are shamefully to betray our allies, sacrifice them to Russia —thereby breaking up the Triple Alliance, or we are to be attacked in common by the Triple Entente for our fidelity to our allies and punished, whereby they will satisfy their jealousy by *joining in totally ruining us.* That is the real naked situation in nuce, which slowly and cleverly set going, certainly by Edward VII, has been carried on, and systematically built up by the disowned conferences between England and Paris and St. Petersburg; finally brought to a conclusion by George V, and set to work. And thereby *the stupidity and ineptitude of our ally is turned into a snare for us.* So the famous 'circumscription' of Germany has finally become a complete fact, despite every effort of our politicians and diplomats to prevent it. *The net has been suddenly thrown over our head,* and England sneeringly reaps the most brilliant success of her persistently prosecuted purely anti-German world-policy, against which we have proved ourselves helpless, while she twists the noose of our political and economic destruction out of our fidelity to Austria, as we squirm isolated in the net. A great achievement which arouses the admiration even *of him who is to be destroyed as its result!* Edward VII is stronger after his death than I am who am still alive! And there have been people who believed that England could be won over or pacified, by this or that puny measure! Unremittingly, unrelentlessly she has pursued her object, with notes, holiday proposals, scares, Haldane, etc., until point was reached. And we walked into the net and even went into the one-ship program in construction with the ardent hope of thus pacifying England! All my warnings, all my pleas were voiced for nothing. Now comes England's so-called gratitude for it! From the dilemma raised by our fidelity to the venerable old Emperor of Austria we are brought into a situation which *offers England the desired pretext for annihilating us* under the hypocritical cloak of justice, namely, of helping France on account of the reputed 'balance of power' in Europe, i. e., playing the card of all the European nations in England's favor against us! This whole business must now be ruthlessly uncovered and the mask of Christian peaceableness publicly and brusquely torn from its face in public, and the pharisaical hypocrisy exposed on the pillory! And our consuls in Turkey and India, agents, etc., must fire the whole Mohammedan world to fierce rebellion against this hated, lying, conscienceless nation of shop-keepers; for if we are to be bled to death, England shall at least lose India."

This hysterical outburst of a man consciously facing destruction portrays the anguish of Wilhelm and is evidence he did not will the war.

William II made the following memorandum on the same day on an article in the London Morning Post on "Efforts Towards Peace":

"The only possible way to ensure or enforce peace is that England must tell Paris and Petersburg—its Allies—to remain quiet (informed historians now know this is entirely true), i. e., neutral, to the Austro-Serbian conflict, then Germany can remain quiet too. But if England continues to remain silent or to give lukewarm assurances of neutrality; that would mean encouragement to its Allies to attack Austro-Germany. Berlin has tried to mediate between Petersburg and Vienna on the appeal of the Czar. But His Majesty silently had already mobilized before the appeal; so that the mediator —Germany—is placed 'en demeure' and his work become illusory. Now only England alone can stop the catastrophe by restraining its Allies, by clearly intimating that—as Sir E. Grey declared—it had nothing to do with the Austro-Serbian conflict, and that if one of its Allies took an active part in the strife it could not reckon on the help of England. *That would put a stop to all war. King George has communicated England's intention to remain neutral to me by Prince Henry.* On the other hand the Naval Staff have this morning —July 30—received a telegram from the German military attache in London, that Sir E. Grey in a private conversation with Prince Lichnowsky, declared that if Germany made war on France, England would immediately attack Germany with a fleet! *Consequently Sir E. Grey says the direct contrary to what his Sovereign communicated to me through my brother"* (an astonishing contradiction) "and places his King in the position of a double-tongued liar vis-a-vis to me."

"The whole war is plainly arranged between England, France and Russia for the annihilation of Germany, lastly through the conversations with Poincaré in Paris and Petersburg, and *the Austro-Serbian strife is only an excuse to fall upon us! God help us in this fight for our existence,* brought about by falseness, lies and poisonous envy!"

This is not the language of a man wishing war. It is a violent outburst of emotion of a man facing unavoidable destruction.

No wonder the Entente leaders did not insist on trying him under Article 227, Versailles Treaty, for the "supreme offense against international morality and the sanctity of treaties."

The terrible offense charged does not describe Wilhelm II. It describes the Russian conspirators, and the Treaty of Versailles, which, with grave international immorality, violated the solemn pledges made to the Germans as a basis of their surrender and the abdication of the Hohenzollerns— *the fourteen points*. The peace of the world will be best promoted by the elimination of this destructive international blunder.

The Attitude of Nicholas

The attitude of Nicholas II must be interpreted in the light of all the disclosures, and it is demonstrated that Nicholas II was not a personality of commanding intelligence, and it is clear, he was vacillating and weak. Nevertheless, it nowhere appears that he was willing to use his great power to cancel the secret contract of 1892, committing Russia to make war on Germany simultaneously with France. It nowhere appears that he hindered or delayed the war preparations of Russia. It does clearly appear that the Russian statesmen in control of the Russian Foreign Office regarded it as a wise piece of strategy to avoid giving publicity to their secret aggressive intentions. It is now known that the peaceful suggestions of the Czar in proposing in 1899 and 1907 the Hague Conventions may be properly classed with the line of strategy to make the world believe the Russian Empire ardently desired international peace, whereas they had secret covenants contemplating war.

Even the Björkoe Treaty, which William II almost extorted from the Czar in favor of peace between Russia, France and Germany, was shown to be contrary to the policy of the Russian Government, because it was abandoned by Russia.

It is impossible to believe that Nicholas did not know of the annual conferences between the Russian General Staff and the French General Staff, and no interpretation of these conferences can leave any manner of doubt as to what the policy was.

It is incredible that the object of the intrigues of Isvolski could have been unknown and not approved by the Czar.

The December, 1913, report of Sazonoff to the Czar pointed out that *it was vital to Russia to control the Dardanelles, and that this could be accomplished only by a general European war. This met with no rebuke.* The Council of February, 1914, in which it was determined *to acquire the Dardanelles through a general European war, was approved by the Czar in writing.*

The Current History of July 26, 1926, (page 559) gives an account of Baron Edmund Heyking (May, 1914) having told Baron Friedrich Rosen, former Foreign Minister of Germany, that he had had a letter from special friends in St. Petersburg about the middle of March, 1914, stating that the Czar had advised the Minister of the Imperial household, Baron Frederick, as follows:

"You had better fully prepare your Department for war, as I shall most certainly go to the front with my army."

It must be remembered that in February, 1914, the Czar had talked freely with the Serbian Minister, who advised the Czar he had 500,000 men available for war, which met the Czar's warmest approval.

The negotiations of Russia with Great Britain for an understanding could not have been unknown to the Czar, as it was a matter of vital importance to know that Great Britain could be relied on in case of a general European war.

The duplicity of Nicholas is shown by the fact that after the Russian Crown Council had ordered mobilization on July 24th, he went through the pretense of inviting William II to act as a mediator with Austria when his own army was in process of active mobilization, a fact which he concealed from William II. Even on July 29, four days after he had permitted the war to be set in motion, he telegraphed William II :

"I fear that *very soon* I shall be unable to resist the pressure exercised upon me, and I shall be forced to take measures that will lead to war."

He had already taken those measures in pursuance of a secret contract.

This was a part of the Russian policy to camouflage the war preparations by peace negotiations.

The telegram of Nicholas of July 29 that William II's conciliatory telegram had a very different tone from the official message of the German Ambassador to Sazonoff was a fiction. No such differences existed, and after he had been solemnly warned by William II against mobilization on July 30, the Czar again ordered general mobilization that very day in a formal manner, and advised William II that—

"the military measures now taking form were decided upon five days ago, and for the reason of defense against the preparations of Austria."

It was a false reason. Austria had only ordered a partial mobilization against Serbia, contemplating only a local movement, following the Serbian mobilization, and Austria had not mobilized against Russia, and had no intention of so doing. Austria was strongly opposed to a European war, but was not willing to let the assassination of the Austrian Crown Prince pass without retaliation.

On July 31 Nicholas wired William:

"It is technically impossible to discontinue our military preparations which have been made necessary by the Austrian mobilization."

This was camouflage to keep William quiet until the avalanche should crush him. It was not technically impossible to stop this general mobilization, and nothing of the sort had been made necessary by the Austrian mobilization.

The dispatches show that the French and Russians were pressing their military preparations with the greatest possible energy. Nicholas was trying to keep William II from making counter preparations, and when William II wired Nicholas demanding a definite answer with regard to the cessation of mobilization, he got no reply, which was a further means of killing time while the Russian mobilization proceeded. It may be true that Nicholas was unable to control the Government of which he was the head, but whether true or false, the will to war is demonstrated to have been in the hearts of the Russian leaders and not in that of the German Kaiser.

It must not be forgotten the wives of Grand Duke Nicholas and Grand Duke Peter on July 22, 1914, completely disclosed the secret preparations and policy of Russia in their conversation with Paléologue at the banquet given to Poincaré at St. Petersburg. They quoted their father, the King of Montenegro, as having wired them that the European war would begin before the end of July. These thoughtless ladies felt quite safe in talking to Paléologue, and telling him that nothing would be left of Germany and Austria, that the war was certain. These ladies knew the secret Russian policy from their husbands, Grand Duke Nicholas and Grand Duke Peter.

Paléologue, the French Ambassador, discloses in his memoirs, with singular unintelligence, this incriminating evidence in detail and with apparent delight, not realizing that it goes strongly to acquit the German leaders and to convict the Russian and French leaders of the *will to war*.

Nicholas II greatly erred and greatly suffered. Let his soul repose in peace.

III. Some Evidence from Belgium

In the reports from the Belgian ministers and chargés d'affaires at Berlin, London, and Paris to the Minister for Foreign Affairs in Brussels, printed by E. S. Mitler & Sons, Berlin, will be found 200 pages of evidence going to show the attitude of the Quai d'Orsay of Paris, of the Foreign Offices of London, and of Berlin to the general effect *that the Berlin Government was very desirous of maintaining peace, that the French Government became increasingly disposed to war as the war powers of Russia and France were expanded and the Entente with Great Britain became dependable.*

For example, the Belgian Minister at Berlin to the Minister for Foreign Affairs of Belgium says, page 184:

"Everyone in *England and France considers the Entente Cordiale* to be a defensive and *offensive alliance against Germany.* * * * It is *the Entente Cordiale* which *has reawakened in France* an idea of *revanche,* which up to then had slumbered. It is *also the Entente Cordiale which is responsible for the state of uneasiness and unrest prevailing in Europe for the last seven years.* * * * For the present it must therefore be considered as approved that the plan of *assisting France in a war against Germany by landing an army of 150,000 English troops was discussed in London.* There is nothing in this calculated to surprise us. *It is the continuation of the singular proposals made some years ago by Colonel Barnardiston to General Ducarne.*"

The Belgian Minister, Guillaume, at Paris to the Belgian Minister for Foreign Affairs, January 16, 1914, says:[1]

[1] Op. cit. p. 169.

"I already had the honor of informing you that it is M. Poincaré, Delcassé, Millerand, and their friends *who have inaugurated and pursued the nationalistic, militaristic, and Chauvinistic policy, the renascence of which we witnessed. Such a policy constitutes a danger for Europe—and also for Belgium. I see in it the greatest peril threatening today the peace of Europe. * * * The attitude adopted by Barthou has provoked a recrudescence of militarism in Germany.*"

The Belgian Minister at Berlin in a long letter on February 20, 1914, quoted the French Ambassador at Berlin, as follows: [1]

"The majority of the Germans and of the French undoubtedly wish to live in peace. But in both countries there is a powerful minority dreaming solely of battles, of wars, of conquest, or revanche. Herein lies the danger; it is like a powder barrel which any rash act may set on fire."

On May 8, 1914, the Belgian Minister Guillaume at Paris quoted to the Belgian Foreign Office an "experienced and highly placed diplomat" as stating: [2]

"If a serious incident should arise one of these days between France and Germany, the statesmen of the two countries will have to arrive at a peaceful solution of the matter within three days or else there will be war.

"One of the most dangerous elements of the present situation is the *return of France to the three years' service;* the latter has been inconsiderately imposed by the military party, and the country is unable to stand it. Before two years have elapsed France will be placed before the alternative *either of abrogating the three years' act or of going to war. * * * The press in both countries is blameworthy.*

[1] Op. cit. p. 173.
[2] Op. cit. p. 181.

The campaign pursued in Germany against the Foreign Legion is exceedingly clumsy, and the tone of the French newspapers is invariably acrimonious and aggressive."

On June 9, 1914, Guillaume wired the Belgian Foreign Office from Paris as follows: [1]

"During the last few days *the press campaign in favor of the principle of the three years' service has been extremely violent.* All sorts of means have been adopted with a view to influencing public opinion. The newspapers have not hesitated to compromise even General Joffre. We have also seen the French Ambassador in St. Petersburg take—contrary to all precedents—an initiative which may prove dangerous for the future of France. *Is it true that the St. Petersburg cabinet pledged France to adopt the three years' service and that the former is today bringing all its influence to bear in order to prevent the abrogation of the law in question?* * * * We must therefore ask ourselves if the attitude of the St. Petersburg cabinet is based on the conviction that *events are imminent which will permit of Russia making use of the instrument placed by her in the hand of her ally."*

The phrase. "Events are imminent" means "war is near". The Belgian Minister Beyens, at Berlin, June 12, 1914, in a dispatch to the Belgian Foreign Office, said: [2]

"Another criticism which can be leveled against the champions of the three years' service in France is that of *perpetually dragging Russia into the discussion*—Russia whose political aims remain a mystery, *who directs the dual alliance solely for her own benefit* and who, likewise, although she is in noways threatened by Germany, *increases her armaments in alarming proportion."*

[1] Op. cit., p. 182.
[2] Op. cit., p. 186.

IV. Some Evidence from London

In great detail and with innumerable quotations, Francis Neilson, a member of the English Parliament, in his work, "How Diplomats Make War," substantially confirms from English records what has been disclosed in the telegrams above quoted; that is, that there was in effect an understanding between Russia, France, and Great Britain with the military and naval details all worked out by repeated conferences of their general staffs and the understanding that Great Britain would co-operate with France in the event of a war with Germany. For example:

"In London, on Saturday, August 1, Lord Lansdowne, Sir Edward Carson, and Mr. Bonar Law hastened to the center of the diplomatic world.[1] Germany had issued orders for the general mobilization of her army and navy; the next day, the Sabbath, to be the first day. Through the long Sabbath all over the Kingdom thousands of feet tramped Channelwards, regiment after regiment with full kit wound through London streets as the bells from tower and steeple called the folk to prayer. Ministers went to a cabinet meeting there and yielded up to the French Ambassador some token of British friendship."

The German mobilization was ordered 5 P. M. Saturday. The English regiments were on the march Sunday morning armed for war.

On August 1 Sir Edward Grey told the German Ambassa-

[1] How Diplomats Make War, p. 293.

dor that Great Britain would not engage to remain neutral, that—

"we must keep our hands free." [1]

The fact was that Grey was not really free but fully committed, not only by the real intent of the agreement with France, but far more by the interests of Great Britain, as he viewed them and Great Britain instantly carried out the commitment under the agreements with France and with Russia.

Telegram 148 from the British Foreign Office, August 2, 1914:

"After the cabinet meeting this morning, I gave M. Cambon the following memorandum:

"I am authorized to give an assurance that *if the German fleet comes into the Channel or through the North Sea* to undertake hostile operations against French coast or shipping, *the British fleet will give all the protection in its power.*

"This assurance is, of course, subject to the policy of His Majesty's government receiving the support of Parliament, and must not be taken as binding His Majesty's government to take any action *until the above contingency of action by the German fleet takes place.*"

So that the Entente was in fact effective, after all, on the certain contingency of action by the German fleet, and Parliament was committed by its own government's acts. This action was equal to agreeing to attack Germany as an ally of France. The interests of Great Britain, however, made it necessary (in Grey's opinion) when a war actually came between France and Germany that Great Britain should fight

[1] How Diplomats Make War, p. 290.

the military rulers of Germany who would have been dangerous to British interests if they had conquered France and dominated western Europe *whether they were responsible for the war or not.*

Mr. Neilson points out (p. 265) :

"News had reached Berlin that Belgium had issued as early as July 24 a mobilization circular, and an undated instruction to Belgian Ambassadors which contained the information they were to give the chancellors as to her 'strengthened peace footing.' "

The Belgian circular of July 24 (the day after Austria made her demand on Serbia) announced that the Belgian Army had already been mobilized and forts near Germany had been put in order for war.

In the circular of the Belgian Foreign Office to its Ambassadors dated *July 24,* was the inclosure heretofore referred to, without date, but necessarily either of that date or of an earlier date, which states :

"All necessary steps to insure respect of Belgian neutrality have nevertheless been taken by the government. *The Belgian Army has been mobilized* and is *taking up such strategic positions* as have been chosen to secure the defense of the country and the respect of its neutrality. The forts of Antwerp and on the Meuse *have been put in* a state of defense."

There can be no manner of doubt as to what the Grey-Cambon letters meant. The complete plan of naval and military strategy had been worked out between the French and British naval and army officers, and on Sunday morning, the very next morning, after Germany ordered her mobilization of Saturday afternoon, British regiments were marching through London to the front fully equipped for war.[1]

A number of members of the British Cabinet, including Lord Morley, John Burns, etc., resigned when they discovered this secret diplomacy.

The French Government immediately offered Belgium military support[2] and the following dispatch from the French Ambassador at Brussels to the French Government explains the relations between France and Belgium:

"The chief of the cabinet of the Belgian Ministry of War has asked the French military attaché *to prepare at once* for the cooperation and contact of French troops with the Belgian Army pending the results of the appeal to the guaranteeing powers now being made. *Orders have* therefore *been given to Belgian provincial governors not to regard movements of French troops as a violation of the frontier.*"

The British troops took their place on the left wing of the French under the plans long before worked out.

The mobilization of the Belgian Army was completed at least the day before the *general mobilization* of the Russian Army began under Sukhomlinoff's order, July 25, about which "he lied" to the Russian Czar when he represented to his sovereign that it was *a partial mobilization*. It was reordered as a general mobilization by Nicholas on July 29 and again on July 30.

In the trial of Sukhomlinoff, Minister of War, at St. Petersburg, by the revolutionary government of Russia,

[1] How Diplomats Make War, p. 295.
[2] Ibid., p. 310.

"Sukhomlinoff *confessed that* after the Czar had received these telegrams from the Kaiser the Czar called the Minister of War up by telephone and *told him to stop the mobilization. At that time the Czar thought the mobilization* was only *partial. It was* really already *general,* a procedure for which the direct authority of the Czar was necessary and had not been given. Sukhomlinoff confessed that *in making the mobilization general he had concealed this from the Czar*; nay, more, that *he did not reveal it to him* in the conversation by telephone. He next admitted that *he promised the Czar to stop the further mobilization* and *not to issue a general mobilization. He hung up the telephone with a false promise* to the Czar, and, he says, *went on with the mobilization.* His fellow-rogue, Januschkevitch, floundering in his testimony and confronted at all times with contradictions, left the stand in the same disgusting and humiliating condition." [1]

If the democracies or peoples of the world continue to permit secret diplomacy with its ambitious intrigue, militarism, commercial imperialism, this World War will not be the last.

The greatest of the English papers, the London Times, March 15, 1915, correctly states the true position with regard to this matter of British participation in the Triple Entente, as follows: [2]

"There are still some Englishmen and Englishwomen *who greatly err* as to the reasons that have forced England to draw the sword. They know that it was Germany's flagrant violation of Belgian neutrality which filled the cup of her indignation and made her people insist on war (sic). They do not reflect that *our honor and our interest must have compelled us to join France and Russia* even if Germany had scrupulously respected the rights of her small neigh-

[1] Bausman, 200; also Oman's Outbreak of the War, 68.
[2] How Diplomats Make War, 336.

bors, and had sought to hack her way into France through the eastern fortresses."

The word "honor" frequently means "interest" in the diplomatic code.

Great Britain was led into the war on the theory *that British interests required co-operation with France and Russia,* a theory upon which Sir Edward Grey had laid the ground by years of naval and military conferences in which every detail of a war on Germany had been carefully outlined. This contention is thoroughly borne out by the new British documents (see Nos. 101, 369). It was Sir Eyre Crowe and Sir Arthur Nicolson who finally forced Grey into the war.

In Entente Diplomacy and the World, Documents 847 and 850 (Exhibit VII), will be found the British Russian Entente plans. (Congressional Record, December 18, 1923.)

These dispatches demonstrate beyond a possibility of doubt that there were secret conventions thoroughly worked out and planned between Russia, France, and Great Britain as to how war should be made on Germany, involving Great Britain sending empty ships into the Baltic Sea for Russia's use against Germany just before the war of 1914 was declared; (Doc. 850) that England should be prepared to fetter the German fleet in the North Sea; that arrangements in the Mediterranean were to be made, and that especial authority to Russian ships to use French and English ports to establish a complete working plan between the navies and the armies of the three countries—Great Britain, Russia, and

France. The limit of space makes it inexpedient to quote these innumerable documents. (See De Siebert.)

The Russian Ambassador, London, June 25, 1914, telegraphed to Sazonoff:[1]

"Grey told me that he was *greatly alarmed* by the false rumors which were *circulating in the German press concerning the contents of the alleged naval convention between England and Russia.* * * * *Grey assured the German Ambassador* * * * *that between England, on the one hand,* and *France and Russia there existed neither an alliance nor a convention* * * * that their negotiations had *never assumed a character directed against Germany nor had they any reference to the so-called 'encircling policy.'* "

On the face of the Cambon-Grey letters was an express disclaimer that either Government was bound by them, but the actual intent and true, common interest against the German Imperial Government is quite clear.

The English honor and interest were both involved. It certainly appears that France, Russia and Great Britain *did have secret conventions;* the conventions *were directed against Germany,* worked out in detail then in *process of execution* and they were in pursuance of *"the encircling policy";* and were carried out on the battlefields and at sea within 60 days.

Three days later Russo-Serbian intrigues led to the murder of Archduke Ferdinand, and the grand drama, with stage fully set, opened to the astonishment and grief of the poor, little common people who pay taxes and die.

[1] Doc. 855, p. 730, Congressional Record.

The secret entente agreements with France and Russia were repeatedly denied by the representatives of the British Foreign Office, who asserted in Parliament that there was no commitment of the British Government to support the French Government in case of a war with Germany.

On March 10 of 1913, Mr. Asquith, replying to a question in the Commons from Lord Hugh Cecil, denied that England was under an—

"obligation arising owing to an assurance given by the ministry in the course of diplomatic negotiations to send a very large armed force out of this country to operate in Europe."

On March 24 he made similar denials in reply to questions from Sir W. Byles and Mr. King.

On April 14 Mr. Runciman, in a speech at Birkenhead, denied "in the most categorical way" the existence of a secret understanding with any foreign power.

On May 3 the Secretary for the Colonies, Mr. Harcourt, declared that he "could conceive no circumstances in which continental operations would not be a crime against the people of this country."

On June 28 the Undersecretary for Foreign Affairs, Mr. Acland, declared publicly that—

"in no European question were we concerned to interfere with a big army."

On July 1 Lord Loreburn, Lord Chancellor from 1906 to 1912, said—

"that any British Government would be so guilty toward our country as to take up arms in a foreign quarrel is more than I can believe."

On April 28, 1914, and again on June 11, Sir Edward Grey confirmed in the House of Commons Mr. Asquith's assertion, made March 11 and 24, 1913, of British freedom from engagements with continental powers.[1]

These disclosures of systematic deceit in the highest places would seem to justify America in receiving the assurances of European diplomats with some reserve.

Lloyd George, five months before the war, said: [2]

"The German Army is vital not merely to the existence of the German Empire, but to the very life and independence of the nation itself, surrounded as Germany is by other nations, each of which possesses arms *about as powerful as her own.*"

On December 23, 1920, Lloyd George said:

"That no one at the head of affairs quite meant war. It was something into which they glided or rather staggered and stumbled."

This is a confession that the Germans did not will the war, but does not exculpate the statesmen of Russia and France who engineered it.

[1] See Neilson; How Diplomats Make War; Morel, Truth and the War, etc.
[2] Daily Chronicle, January 1, 1914.

CHAPTER VI

THE GREAT REVISION

I. Disinterested French Opinion

A very large number of intellectual Frenchmen, historians, scholars, and soldiers have signed "an appeal to conscience", demanding the modification of Article 231 of the Treaty of Versailles, on the ground that the confession that the German Government was exclusively responsible for the war was extorted by violence, and has no binding force in morals or ethics. A number of these men have written books demonstrating the untruth of the charge, to whom a previous reference has been made. Some of their works will be found cited in the Appendix. These men are typical of the France Americans have so greatly admired. Their counsel does great honor to France.

It may be well to quote a few expressions from the writings and speeches of some of these men.

Victor Margueritte has recently written a notable book called "Les Criminels" in which he traces Poincaré's steps and shows by the evidence that he willed the war, and took

[1] See Appendix.

a strenuous part in bringing it about; that his repeated assurances to the Russian authorities of support of the Russian policy in the Balkans, and in making war on Germany stimulated the Russian Imperialists to attack Germany in reliance on French and British co-operation.

On July 5, 1922, page 2337, Journal Official, Vaillant-Couturier while M. Poincaré was presiding over the Chamber of Deputies as its President, declared to his fellow deputies "upon his conscience as an old soldier" that he was convinced of the responsibility of Raymond Poincaré for the World War, and that the records would expose the fact. He accused him of unwarrantably supporting the Russian ambitions and policies; declared that Poincaré did not do what he could have done to deter the war, but promoted it, and built up in France public opinion favorable to Russian intervention in the Balkans, and he said:

"We accuse him of having been the man about whom was crystallized the desire for revenge on the part of the most turbulent of French nationalists. We accuse him of having been that which Jaurés hoped he would not be, the president of reaction or of war.

"We accuse him of having let pass certain omissions of texts in the publication of the diplomatic archives. * * *

"We accuse him of having thrown France into a war which the Russian mobilization provoked. * * *

"For us M. Poincaré represents all that nationalism has been able to produce of a funereal character before, during and after the war. To-day his policy leads us to isolation, to failure, and to new wars."

Even the former Russian Minister of War who co-operated with Poincaré (Sukhomlinoff) is quoted:

"I dare say that the belief in the sole guilt in Germany is not possible even to M. Poincaré. But if one can conduct a policy of extortion which is based upon the theory of Germany's sole guilt, it is clear that one should grimly stick to this theory, or at least give oneself the appearance of conviction."

This advice to be a judicious hypocrite appears to have been fully appreciated by Poincaré. It must be remembered that in ascertaining the actual truth, it is necessary to remember that the public expressions in favor of peace and justice and right by men like Poincaré and Sazonoff and Sukhomlinoff can only be interpreted in the secret agreements, records, dispatches, etc., which were not made public, and which flatly contradicted their pacific pretensions.

For example, Poincaré published in England on the 31st of July a letter to the King of England urging him to try to preserve the peace, and stating that France would do its utmost to do likewise, after his own Government had caused a secret telegram to be sent to St. Petersburg saying that the French Government was firmly determined on war (Telegram 216), and although the secret treaty between Russia and France had already committed both France and Russia absolutely and unequivocally to attack Germany immediately without further notice. Such official hypocrisy would make it impossible to know the truth except for the secret records which have recently been disclosed.

Some of the opinions of distinguished Frenchmen who love and honor France, who wish France to be honored by other nations, and who remember that the French Government can only be honored and loved in such degree as it is honest and just to other people, are here recorded—

Deschanel, former President of France:

"Poincaré provoked the war because the adherents of the three-year military service proposition had an interest in anticipating the opponents of the law in their efforts to abolish it. * * * Poincaré knew we were not prepared, yet he went to Petersburg for the purpose of driving the Russians into war."[1]

Gouttenoire de Toury, in "Poincaré a-t-il voulu la Guerre?":

"The Treaty was the work of hatred, of falsehood and of violence. Our united duty is to combat this hatred, this falsehood, this violence, in the interest of truth and peace, and relentlessly to put down the Versailles Treaty and especially Article 231."

Louis Guétant in "Rapport sur le Traité de Versailles":

"With all our troubles over the present, the responsibility for the war remains the greatest distress of our soul; it continues to be the question of questions, for upon the answer depends the whole effect and legality of the Treaty, and with that our future. We cannot permit that the Treaty of Versailles should pass as a work founded upon violence, which will challenge the repugnance of all honest men and harbors the seeds of future wars. We can uproot this cursed seed only by demanding the revision of the treaty. This is a categorical imperative, the duty of conscience and of self-preservation."

General Percin, former Inspector General of the French Artillery, in an Article in the Ere Nouvelle:

[1] From Letters to the French Ambassador, George Louis, in St. Petersburg, February 22, 1915, and June 26, 1915.

"In order to effect an understanding between the two peoples, the first duty is to break down the moral barrier which has been erected against Germany by the Treaty of Versailles and the French post-war propaganda, the lies about Germany's guilt during the war as well as of causing the war."

Alfred Pevet in "Les Responsables de la Guerre" ·

"And so seventy million Germans at the end of the war, rendered impotent for defense by starvation, have signed a treaty, intended to make them weak and weaponless for centuries and to reduce them to a refined state of slavery. By means of loaded dice the defenders of human rights have been able to bring a great nation to the point of prostrating itself before men and gods by signing this Article 231 :"

Victor Margueritte in "Les Criminels":

"The real workers for war, the principals responsible for the whole-sale murder, are Poincaré and Viviani, the one as Minister-President, a helpless shadow, the other as President of the French Republic, mightier than the Russian Czar, yet a puppet in the hands of Isvolski. These men, in intimate conjunction with the war party at the Russian Court, are responsible for the catastrophe. In the interest of justice as well as of peace the harm caused by Article 231 which was ex-torted from the vanquished under threats of war and starvation and as a confession of sole guilt, must be righted.   Therefore this Article 231 must be revised, the sooner the better, if there is to be a moral disarmament between us and Germany, a real peace and an enduring European reconciliation. The extorted confession of guilt is drowned by one demand: the demand for new facts."

Fabre Luce in "La Victoire":

"In reality Germany and Austria did only what might make war possible; the Triple Entente did what made war certain. In the wish to form a Defensive Alliance against Germany, France welded together an Alliance of Conquerors."

Alfred Ebray, former French Consul General and Minister-Resident, in "La Paix Malpropre":

"The confession of guilt was forced from the vanquished after the methods employed in medieval juridical proceedings, having no legality either morally, politically or historically, and therefore valueless in a careful investigation of the responsibility for the war."

Georges Demartial, former Director of the French Colonial Ministry:

"Our imperative duty today is to go back into the past, since the future depends upon the past. More than ever, the war guilt question is the question of all questions. It not only raises the greatest conceivable moral problem, but the world's destiny depends upon its solution. Not until Article 231 of the Versailles Treaty has been revised will justice be done to a lie of the past. The Treaty of Versailles is a treaty of violence, and nothing else. Its object is to punish Germany for causing the war. It follows that it is valid in the degree that it is true that Germany's adversaries were forced to take part in the war. But if it shall be proved that Germany's adversaries are equally guilty or more guilty than Germany, the treaty will fall of its own weight, since it is founded solely upon their assertion of complete innocence."

Professor Renouvin, in "Les Origines Immediates de la Guerre":

"Article 231 pronounces a judgment: With insufficient evidence the statesmen have undertaken to lay down an official conviction, to interpret a historical fact which in its very character is lacking in scientific details."

A REMARKABLE ARTICLE

By M. GEORGES DEMARTIAL

Officer of the Legion of Honor, Honorary Minister General of Colonies has just appeared (Feb. 1927).

The Treaty of Versailles has declared the defeated countries to be alone responsible for the war. The truth about guilt is not sufficiently proved by this declaration. On the contrary, very strong reasons for doubting the veracity of the above charge emerge when one examines the principal arguments upon which this belief is still based.

It is said that the central empires had alone prepared for the war.

During the ten years which preceded the war, Russia, France and England had set aside in their budgets for military expenses 46,000,000,000 francs, whereas the central empires had set aside 26,000,000,000 francs.

It is said that the policies of the governments of the Entente were pacific.

In 1915 the Germans seized in Brussels and published 119 reports addressed to the Belgian government by its ministers in London, Paris and Berlin, between the years 1905 and 1914.

This is how one publication, otherwise very Francophile, *The Revue de Lausanne,* summarized these reports when they appeared:

"The Belgian diplomats endeavor to prove that the foreign policy of France, and especially that of England, is dangerous to the peace of Europe."

In February, 1919, the Soviet government of Russia published in the *Pravda* the correspondence exchanged from 1908 to 1914 between the Russian ambassadors in London and in Paris, and their governments. Professor Pokroksky, people's commissar, in charge of this publication, says: "All these documents expose in the fullest manner the activities of the Entente in preparing for the war."

It is said that Serbia was innocent.

This was not the opinion held by the English at the beginning of the war. Here is what may be read in newspapers of the most widely different shades of belief:

"If one could tow Serbia to the edge of the ocean and swamp it, the atmosphere of Europe would be cleared." (*Manchester Guardian,* Aug. 3.)

"Serbia ought to disappear. Let us efface it from the map of Europe." (John Bull, Aug. 8.)

The English minister of foreign affairs himself had said to the ambassador of Austria on July 27: "If it is possible for Austria to make war on Serbia and at the same time to give satisfaction to Russia, everything would be fine." (English Diplomatic Documents, V. 1, number 40.)

It is said that the Serbian government could not have accepted the Austrian note without dishonor to herself.

Nevertheless, the Italian government suggested to the Eng-

[1] Translated by Arthur Julius Nelson.

lish government on July 27 to advise Serbia to accept it. (English Diplomatic Documents, V. I, number 48.) On the next day, the 28th, the Italian government resumed its suggestion in the same manner; the Serbian chargé d'affaires had informed it that his government would be ready to accept the note in its entirety if some explanations of articles 5 and 6 were furnished him; the explanation, in this respect, given by Austria to the powers in her memorandum of July 27, appeared to him to be precisely of a nature to facilitate Serbia's acceptance. (English Diplomatic Documents, V. I, number 64.)

It is to be noted that this memorandum has not been published in the diplomatic books of the Entente.

It is said that by refusing arbitration, the Central Powers put themselves under the ban of humanity.

Would a Russian, French, or English government have accepted it any the more? Why should Austria not have employed force against Serbia in 1914, since Serbia had used it in 1912 against Turkey, and in 1913 against Bulgaria? The offer is lost at the end of Serbia's reply, and is incidentally made in a personal telegram from the Czar to the Kaiser, which the Russian government kept secret for six months. It was mentioned but once, that is all. It was never mentioned again. The governments of the Entente never considered it in the course of negotiations. Why did they not solemnly declare that they were henceforward decided, if Austria accepted arbitration, not to wage war any more against any nation, small or large? That was the time to preach by example, or never.

It is said that Emperor William, a modern Attila, personally schemed to bring about this war in order to gorge his people with booty.

On July 28 the emperor received a copy of the Serbian reply to the Austrian note. He inserted these words: "To have attained these results in 48 hours is wonderful. It is more than was to be expected. It is a great moral victory for Vienna. But now every motive for war disappears, and the Austrian minister could well have remained in Belgrade. Under such conditions, I myself should never have ordered the mobilization against Serbia." (Kautsky Documents, number 271.) And he wrote immediately to the minister of foreign affairs and presented him with a suitable plan of instructions for his ambassador at Vienna. (Kautsky Documents, number 293.)

It is said that the German government never desired to give a counsel of moderation to Austria.

On July 28, while carrying out precisely this wish of the Kaiser, the German government telegraphed to Vienna: "The Serbian reply contains such concessions to the Austrian demands, that if the Austrian government maintains an uncompromising attitude, it will have to expect to see the public opinion of all Europe turn progressively against it." (Kautsky Documents, number 323.) From this moment onward he urged Austria to come to an understanding with Russian and to accept England's offer of mediation. Better still, in order that his efforts should not be wasted, he had recourse to an extraordinary proceeding: he published in an English newspaper, the *Westminster Gazette,* on Aug. 1, the text of one of his most condemnatory dispatches to Vienna.

It is said that the general mobilization was simply a precautionary measure, lacking any belligerent motives, and that in calling upon Russia to suspend it, Germany simply found a pretext for declaring war on her.

In Number 71 of the Yellow Book on the Franco-Russian alliance, there is related a conversation of Aug. 18, 1892, between General de Boisdeffre, the French negotiator, and the Czar, on the subject of Article 3 of the military treaty, by which the two powers engaged themselves to mobilize immediately if Germany or Austria mobilized against one of them.

"I remarked to the emperor that mobilization was a declaration of war," said the general.

"That is the sense in which I understand it," replied the emperor. Why should Germany have understood otherwise?

It is said that the general Russian mobilization was a counter stroke to the general Austrian mobilization.

On Sept. 15, 1917, the Russian government, at that time represented by Kerensky, made known, in an official communiqué, that the order for general mobilization was announced in Russia on the evening of July 30, 1914, and no one has placed the general mobilization order of Austria befor July 31. But long before the Kerensky communiqué, the truth was known.

It is said that France and England did not want war.

Between the moment when the Russian general mobilization order was made public (the night of the 30th and 31st) and the declaration of war by Germany on Russia (Aug. 1, 7 p. m.) sufficient time elapsed for the governments to demand that Russia stop a mobilization which was an act of war.

It is said that in reality if France entered the war, it was solely in order to resist Germany's aggression; without this aggression, there would not have been any war.

In his great speech on the afternoon of Aug. 3, the English minister of foreign affairs, Sir Edward Grey, proclaimed in the House of Commons:

"I may say with the most absolute certainty that the French are involved in the war on account of an obligation of honor resulting from a definite alliance with Russia."

Germany did not declare war on France until the evening of the day on which these words were uttered. Germany's declaration of war was, therefore, posterior to France's entrance into the war; it was the effect, not the cause.

It is said that Germany's aggression against France was the greatest crime that a civilized country has ever committed against international law.

In Foignet's Manual of International Law we read: "In the relations between the ally of one of the belligerents and the other belligerent, one of two things may occur. Either the ally will attack the belligerent in carrying out its treaty of alliance, or the ally will maintain an indecisive attitude, awaiting the issue of the first encounters. In the latter case, the belligerent if it knows of the existence of the treaty of alliance, and if it feels strong enough, may attack the ally of its enemy, after a preliminary declaration of war." (P. 490.) Since manuals are only the résumé of what many precedents teach this theory ought to be applicable. In attacking France, therefore, Germany committed no crime; she followed the rules of the game.

It is said that this attack took France by surprise, that it was made in a treacherous manner.

This attack was not a surprise to any one. It was made known everywhere that in case of a war waged simultaneously against France and Russia, it would be a necessity of life or death for Germany to try to defeat one of her adversaries as soon as possible so that she could then direct all her forces against the other, and that the adversary she would attack first would be France.—The French government was so little surprised by Germany's attack, that it deliberately exposed itself to it. On July 29 and 30, nearly a week before the declaration of war, the French ambassador reported to the Foreign Office, "that France was expecting Germany to demand of her, either to stop her preparations or to issue a declaration of neutrality, and that, since France could not accede of these demands, Germany would attack her." (English Documents, V. 1, numbers 89 and 105.)

It is said that in holding her troops at a distance of ten kilometers from the front, the French government gave most decisive proof that it did not want war and made the supreme sacrifice in the cause of peace.

But since the general Russian mobilization was equivalent to a declaration of war on Germany, and since France was engaged, as a matter of honor, to aid Russia, this withdrawal was only a bluff; it was not a sacrifice, since on the avowal of Mr. Viviani himself in his speech of Jan. 31, 1919, the general staff, on being consulted, had raised no objection. The withdrawal did not change the course of events at all, and could not have changed it. It did not prevent Sir Edward Grey from confessing, on Aug. 3, that France was engaged in the war by virtue of her alliance with Russia.

It is said that England entered the war only to protect the neutrality of Belgium.

It is true that in his great speech on Aug. 6, Mr. Asquith, after asking the question: Why is England fighting? solemnly declared that it was for this reason, and no other; and he added specifically: "We are not fighting for selfish interests." But the famous leader in the *Times* of March 8, following, was devoted wholly to demonstrating that "England would certainly have joined France and Russia even if Germany had respected the neutrality of Belgium, that she did not intend to play the part of an international Don Quixote, and that if she had entered the war, it was because her interests were involved, interests which called upon her to fight Germany, as she had fought Philip II, Louis XIV and Napoleon I."

Here, apart from reasons based upon conscience and common sense, is a brief summary, of a documentary nature, of the reasons why we should refuse to place all responsibility

for the war on Germany. It seems, now that this corner of
the veil has been raised, that the League of the Rights of
Man should endeavor to remove it entirely. It was formed a
quarter of a century ago, in order to obtain the revision of
a judgment rendered contrary to the essential rules of justice.
It ought to demand to-day the revision of Article 231 of the
Treaty of Versailles, by which the several enemies of Germany compelled her, without debate, despite her protestations,
and under stress of having hostilities resumed against her in
five days, to assume sole responsibility for the war. Since
it is on this admission that the whole treaty has been erected,
and especially the chapter on reparations, the question is
important.

II. Some Very Late Authorities

There have just been published in English some new
books by four different authors of great distinction, an
American, an Englishman, a Frenchman, a German, which
confirm the verity of the story disclosed in this volume.

"International Anarchy" by G. Lowes Dickinson (Century
Company of Oxford), a masterpiece of the first order by
an Englishman (500 pages); a historical demonstration of
the truth and a philosophical discussion of the best possible
type.

"The Limitations of Victory" by Alfred Fabre-Luce (A.
A. Knopf). Fabre-Luce is a Frenchman, a historian who is
judicious, impartial, whose one great motive is the truth.

He has demolished the defenses and pretenses of Raymond Poincaré.

"Isvolski and the World War" by Frederick Stieve (A. A. Knopf). Frederick Stieve is a German of vast learning, whose book on Isvolski must be convincing to any impartial mind. Stieve has edited all of the dispatches, letters and documents proceeding from Isvolski, and is the highest authority on the secret documents of Russia.

Finally, "The Genesis of the World War" by Harry Elmer Barnes, Professor of Historical Sociology, Smith College, etc., a work whose brilliancy and power is not surpassed by any recent piece of historical writing. Its scholarship, its literary excellence, its rhetorical and logical arrangement, its tremendous accumulation of effective data make this work a great masterpiece.

Professor Barnes, with additional evidence, draws the same substantial conclusions as those presented to the United States Senate on December 18, 1923, by Mr. Owen, Senator from Oklahoma.

He says:

That previous to the outbreak of the World War, the most important point in Russian foreign policy was the securing of the Straits, and that they could only be obtained by a European war: that Sazonoff was converted to this view and expressed himself as believing that, with British help, France and Russia could easily dispose of Germany and put an end to her existence as a first-class European power: that a secret Russian Crown Council, held on February 8, 1914, decided that Russia must await a European war: that English adherence to the Franco-Russian plans was practically assured by the negotiations concerning an Anglo-Russian naval convention in May, 1914:

That Poincaré had assured Isvolski in 1912 that as soon as Russia was adequately prepared in a military way, and the bribed French press had reconciled the French people to the idea of a war over the Balkans, he would join with Russia in any satisfactory incident in the Balkans which might be used as the basis for precipitating the war which would restore Alsace-Lorraine, as well as capture the Straits. That the Russians had therefore encouraged Serbian plots against Austria, supplied the Serbians with arms, and promised them Russian aid against Austria:

That Poincaré visited St. Petersburg late in July, 1914, fired the Russian militarists with new zeal and hope, and gave the Russian extremists assurance of full support against Austria before he knew the terms of the Austrian ultimatum, and gave them to understand that the prospective Austro-Serbian crisis would be satisfactory to him as the "Incident in the Balkans" over which the Russians might kindle a European war and count upon finding France a reliable ally. Hence, that while Russia brought on the war, she would never have done so but for prior incitement by Poincaré:

That from the 24th of July, the Russians began steady and unabated military preparations in anticipation of war, and carried these to their logical and fatal culmination in the general mobilization order of July 30. That the 24th of July marks the turning point in the history of contemporary Europe which transformed the European system from one which invited war into one which was based upon a determination to precipitate war. That neither the French nor the British offered any objections to these Russian military measures, and the French explicitly advised greater haste, coupled with more complete secrecy. That consciously or unconsciously, on July 25, Sir Edward Grey led Sazonoff to understand that Great Britain would countenance Russian mobilization.

That personal responsibility for the deadly Russian military preparations rests mainly upon the Grand Duke Nicholas, Sazonoff and Isvolski, but chiefly on Sazonoff, who led the militarists on rather than being bulldozed by them.

That in 1916 Sazonoff admitted that the war was brought on in 1914 through the determination of France and Russia to humiliate Germany. That his recent attempt to clear himself of the charges against him, have consisted solely of the most obvious and flagrant misstatements of easily verified and incontestable facts. That he has not been able to offer one valid fact in extenuation of his conduct.

That Sazonoff's suggestions as to a diplomatic settlement were not made in good faith, but, following the suggestions of the Protocol of 1912, were designed purely to gain more time for the execution of the Russian military preparations.

The German and Austrian military action against Russia came long after the Russian general mobilization, and

neither country had made a move against Russia until after
the Russian general mobilization order had been telegraphed
throughout Russia. That Germany did not even then move
hastily, but vainly waited twenty-four hours for a reply to a
twelve-hour ultimatum to Russia before ordering mobilization. (Genesis of the World War, 371.)

III. Professor Barnes' Conclusions With Regard to
the Attitude of the Russian and French Leaders
in Precipitating the World War [1]

"The problem of responsibility for the World War is not
primarily an abstract matter for scholarly meditation, but is
rather one of the livest and most important practical issues
of the present day. The whole European situation rests
to a large extent upon unwise and unjust treaties of peace
which grew out of the most complete and uncritical acceptance of the grossest forms of wartime illusions created by
the Entente propaganda concerning the responsibility for
the World War. The discovery and dissemination of the
facts concerning the outbreak of the war are not only indis-
pensable to the problem of eliminating the injustices of the
Treaties of Versailles, St. Germain and Trianon, but are
also of vital significance in promoting the cause of world
peace and firm international organization.

"For the first time in the history of mankind the genera-

[1] This summary of Professor Barnes' views was specially revised
for citation in this book.

tion that lived through a great war has been enabled to obtain the information upon which may be based a definite
knowledge of the causes and responsibility for that war.
Hitherto, states have kept secret the documents in the
foreign offices which revealed the facts as to war guilt.
Rarely have such documents been published until from forty
to one hundred years after the event. For example, in 1914
we possessed no complete documentary knowledge of the
causes of and responsibility for the Franco-Prussian war
of 1870. The reasons for our peculiar advantages at the
present time are clear. In Germany, Austria and Russia the
governments in power during the World War were over-
thrown and supplanted by new ones. The latter desired to
make their status and power more permanent in every possible way, and believed that this could be done in part by discrediting the previous régimes.

"One method of discrediting the earlier governments would
be to show, if possible, that they were responsible for the
tragedies and miseries incident to the World War. This led
to the opening of the secrets of the foreign offices in Germany, Austria and Russia, and the subsequent publication of
the relevant documents under competent editorship. The
German and Austrian documents give us extensive knowledge about the relation of the central powers to the outbreak of the war, and the fact that Russia was closely allied
with France and England not only makes the Russian documents of significance with respect to Russia herself but also
gives us most of the essential information with respect to

the policies and acts of the French and English governments in the crisis of July and August, 1914. The British government itself has recently consented to the publication of the secret documents in its own archives, and we now possess this information on the crisis of 1914 in carefully edited form. Serbia, France and Italy must stand self-condemned until they freely open their archives to scholars.

"Thus the revolutionary transformation of the attitude of scholars toward the responsibility for the World War has not in any sense been due to a mere swinging of the psychological pendulum away from the ardent hatred of Germany during the World War, or to the progress of German propaganda since 1918, but has inevitably grown out of the fact that today we have real knowledge of the situation, while from 1914-1918 we were guided solely by the propaganda of the governments which closely guarded the secrets with respect to the actual responsibility for the great calamity. There is nothing mysterious or esoteric about this new information or its sources. Practically all of the source material has at the present time been published and any industrious person could easily read it all through and digest it in a few weeks if adequately oriented in modern diplomatic history. It would certainly be a crime of omission of the first magnitude if scholars were not to exploit this unique opportunity to destroy the dangerous and menacing war psychology of hatred and myth and supplant it by the solid and substantial body of fact and understanding which is now at our disposal.

"The general European system after 1870, based as it was on nationalism, militarism, secret alliances and imperialistic aims, naturally inclined Europe toward war. For the existence of this situation all the European countries must share the responsibility. The European system does not, however, explain why war came in 1914, as the same general European situation had been prevailing for many years prior to that time, though certain problems had become more acute in the years immediately preceding the World War, particularly in the Near East and Morocco.

"The Franco-Russian Alliance concluded by 1894 was transformed into an offensive organization following 1912 through the co-operation of Isvolski and Poincaré. Both recognized that the chief objectives of Russian and French foreign policy, the seizure of the Straits and the return of Alsace-Lorraine, could be realized only through a general European war. From 1912-14 their joint plans, which were successfully executed, involved: (1) a manipulation of the Balkan situation in such a fashion as to be able to take advantage of any crisis likely to provoke a European war; (2) an arrangement to get England so involved that she would be bound to come in on the side of France and Russia; and (3) a great increase in the military preparations of France and Russia. France loaned Russia large sums of money for armaments and strategic railroads, while Russian money was sent in great quantities to Paris to bribe the French newspapers to support the policies of Isvolski and Poincaré.

"It was decided that Serbia would be the most favorable

area in which to create the desired crisis in the Balkans. Hence, Serbian nationalism was strongly encouraged and directed particularly against the position of Austria in the Balkans. In February 1914, the Czar received the premier of Serbia, offered encouragement to the Serbian plans, and promised arms and ammunition to Serbia for the impending European war. In February 1914, the Russians in a secret crown council, decided upon the steps to be taken as soon as the European war broke out. In the early spring of 1914 Dragutin Dimitrievitch, a prominent officer in the Serbian general staff exploited and brought to fruition a plot for the assassination of the Austrian Archduke Franz Ferdinand. The Serbian civil government and Royal Family were aware of the plot for nearly a month before its execution, but made no adequate effort to stop the plot or to warn Austria. Prominent Russians were also aware of the plot, but the degree of the complicity of Russia is as yet uncertain. At least we know that the Russian minister and military attaché in Belgrade both knew of the plot and approved its execution. The military attaché gave 8000 francs (presumably secured from Russia) to the plotters for the expenses of the assassination.

"When the assassination came, the French and Russians recognized that the impending clash between Austria and Serbia would constitute a highly appropriate episode over which to bring about the desired European conflict. The year 1914 was a particularly desirable year for the Entente because there was imminent danger that England might develop more happy relations with Germany, and that the French Radicals might be able to secure the repeal of the French army law of 1913. Russia was threatened by an economic revolution which a war was sure to avert. Further, France had four classes with the colors in the spring of 1914. Poincaré went to St. Petersburg late in July, 1914, and, before knowing the terms of the Austrian ultimatum, renewed his pledge of November 17, 1912 to support Russia in a war over the Balkans, and indicated that the probable Austro-Serbian conflict would meet the conditions demanded by the French in supporting Russia in intervention in the Balkans.

"The Franco-Russian procedure in 1914, already outlined by these powers as early as the fall of 1912, was to advocate a show of conciliation and concessions on the part of Serbia, and to indicate apparent Franco-Russian willingness to settle the dispute through diplomacy while secret Franco-Russian military preparations were to be carried on which would ultimately make a diplomatic adjustment impossible. Hence, Russia urged Serbia not to declare war on Austria, and, to insure a sufficiently conciliatory Serbian reply to Austria, the Serbian response to the Austrian ultimatum was drafted in outline by Philippe Berthelot in the French foreign office. Russia did not desire to have Serbia precipitate matters prematurely by an early declaration of war on Austria, because this would have affected European opinion unfavorably, particularly English opinion and would also have brought about military activities altogether too rapidly for Russia, whose mobilization over a vast area would necessarily be slow as compared with that of Austria and Germany. The Serbian reply to Austria was cleverly phrased so as to appear to concede much, while actually conceding nothing of vital importance. It was skillfully designed to invite further Austrian aggression against Serbia, but also to discredit such aggression before European opinion. Indeed, it was so adroitly executed that it deceived even the Kaiser, who believed it an adequate reply to the Austrian demands.

"On July 24, the moment Russia and France learned of the terms of the Austrian ultimatum to Serbia, they began that dual programme of a diplomatic barrage combined with secret military preparations which had made a European war inevitable by the afternoon of July 30. Baron Schilling tells us in his authoritative diary that the moment Sazonov read the Austrian ultimatum to Serbia on July 24 he exclaimed: 'This means the European war!' Dobrorolski likewise frankly confesses that the Russian army circles regarded the European war as inevitable from the 24th onward, and worked steadily to prepare for it with the greatest possible expedition. Russia sent a diplomatic message to Serbia on the 24th counselling moderation, but at the same time decided upon the mobilization of the four great military districts of central and southern Russia as well as of the two Russian fleets. Russian money in Germany and Austria was also called in. On the same day Viviani telegraphed to the French foreign office that the Austro-Serbian situation was likely to create serious European complications, and the French troops in Morocco were ordered home. On the 25th the Russian Crown Council and military authorities decided on war. Both countries began systematic military preparations for the war on July 26.

"By July 28, the time had come when Russian military preparations had gone far enough to warrant a general mobilization and the Tsar was persuaded to consent to this order during July 29. A telegram from the Kaiser, however, induced him to revoke the order, but on the 30th Sazonov and the army officials once more extorted from the Tsar his reluctant consent to the order for general mobilization. As soon as Sazonov had overcome the Tsar's resistance he ran downstairs, telephoned to Januskhevich, the chief of staff, told him to hand the mobilization order to Dobrorolski, and ordered him then to smash his telephone and keep out of sight for the rest of the day, so that he could not be found if anything should induce the Tsar to change his mind again about the mobilization policy. Baron Schilling tells us that great enthusiasm prevailed among the Russians over this fatal decision on general mobilization.

"The French and the Russians had understood for a generation that once Russian general mobilization was ordered there would be no way to prevent a general European war. General Dobrorolski has told us with great candor that both the Russian military and civil authorities in 1914 fully realized that a European war was on as soon as the mobilization order had been sent out of the general telegraph office in St. Petersburg late in the afternoon of July 30. To use Dobrorolski's own words: 'This (the general mobilization order) once decided there is no way backwards. This step settles automatically the beginning of war. The order was known in all the larger towns of our huge country. No change was possible. The prologue of the great historic drama had begun.'

"The French authorities had been thoroughly informed as to the nature and progress of the Russian military preparations, but they made no effort to restrain them, though the French knew well that these military activities were bound to render a European war inevitable. After a secret meeting late on July 29, Poincaré and his ministers actually urged the Russians to speed up their military preparations, but to be more cautious about them, so as not to alienate England or to provoke Germany to counter-mobilization. On the night of July 31 the French Government went still further and openly decided for war, handing this information to Isvolski with great enthusiasm and high spirits about midnight of the 31st. France was, thus, the first country to declare itself for war in the European crisis of 1914.

"The Austrian statesmen in 1914 decided that the time had come when it was absolutely necessary to curb the Serbian menace, and they consciously planned an ultimatum to Serbia of such severity that it would be practically impossible for Serbia to concede all of the Austrian demands. The plan then, was to make a show of diplomacy but to move toward a certain punitive war; This program was much like that of France and Russia, save for the vital difference that Austria decided to provoke nothing but a local punitive war while the plans of France and Russia envisaged a general European conflict. This is the most important point to be borne in mind when estimating the relative war guilt of Austria as against that of France and Russia. Russia had no moral basis for the assumed rôle of the protector of the Serbs in 1914. It had been Russia who suggested the annexation of Bosnia and Herzegovina in 1908. Even more significant, in the autumn of 1911 Russia proposed to Turkey that she would protect Turkey against the Slavic peoples of the Balkans if Turkey would open the Straits to Russia. The British Ambassador in Paris in 1914 designated "as mere rubbish" the Russian pretensions as protectress of all the Slavic peoples.

"The Hungarian premier, Count Tisza, was thoroughly opposed to war and did all he could to force the Austrian ministers to adopt a policy towards Serbia which would be the least likely to provoke a general European war. Tisza was the most pacific statesman of 1914 in the Austro-Hungarian-Dual-Monarchy. Hungary cannot be said to have any immediate responsibility for the outbreak of the war in 1914.

"Germany, formerly friendly to Serbia, was alarmed by the assassination of the Archduke and the resulting menace to her chief ally. Germany therefore at first agreed on July 6th to stand behind Austria in the plan of the latter to exe, cute her programme of punishing Serbia, and urged Austria to move rapidly in the situation. The answer of the Serbians to the Austrian ultimatum, however, impressed the

Kaiser as satisfactory, and from that time on he was strongly opposed to military activity on the part of Austria against Serbia. He cancelled his blank check to Austria long before the Russian mobilization. In co-operation with Sir Edward Grey, Germany began on July 27, to urge upon Austria the opening of direct negotiations with Russia and the mediation of her dispute with Serbia. Austria at first refused to listen to this advice and declared war upon Serbia on the 28th. Germany became still further alarmed at the rumored Russian military preparations, and vigorously pressed Austria for a diplomatic settlement of the dispute. Germany rejected only one of the five diplomatic methods proposed for the settlement of the crisis of 1914, and for this she offered as a substitute a plan which Grey himself admitted was a better scheme than the one rejected.

"Austria did not give way and consent to direct negotiations with Russia concerning Serbia until July 31, which was too late to avert a general European war, because the Russian mobilization was then in full swing. Germany endeavored without success to secure the suspension of military activities by Russia, and then, after unexpected hesitation and deliberation, declared war upon Russia.

"The Russian general mobilization, undertaken with the full connivance of the French, was ordered at a time when diplomatic negotiations were moving rapidly towards a satisfactory settlement of the major problems in the crisis, and when England and Germany were in full agreement as to the trend of negotiations. Hence the Russian general mobilization was an unjustifiable act of aggression which not only initiated military hostilities, but was also the chief reason for the failure of the diplomatic efforts. Before the Russian mobilization was ordered the Austrian ambassador in St. Petersburg repeatedly assured Sazonov that Austria would respect the sovereignty and territorial integrity of Serbia, and Sazonov agreed that he was convinced on this point, though he concealed these Austrian assurances from his colleagues. Any diplomatic advantage which Russia desired to gain from mobilization could have been gained by a partial mobilization which would not have necessitated German military intervention. Sazonov, however, sharply refused to sanction this plan.

"England was for peace provided France was not drawn into the conflict, but Grey was absolutely determined to come into the war in case France was involved. As France decided from the beginning to stand with Russia for war, and as Grey refused to attempt to restrain either France or Russia, England was inevitably drawn away from her encouragement of the German efforts towards a diplomatic settlement of the crisis and into acquiesence in the military agression of France and Russia. Grey made his decision to enter the war before Belgium had been invaded, and after Germany had proposed to keep out of Belgium and to refrain from attacking France if England would remain neutral. In fact Lichnowsky even suggested that Germany might guarantee the integrity of France and the French colonies in the event of war if England would promise neutrality. The Belgian issue in England was, then, a pure subterfuge, exploited by Grey to inflame British opinion against Germany and to secure British support of his war policy. Grey was brought to intervene in part by the pressure of his subordinates Nicholson and Crowe.

"The United States entered the war in part because the British blockade of the ports of the Central Powers led us to have our chief financial and commercial stake in the Entente, and partly because of the pro-British sympathies of Ambassador Page and President Wilson, which made it impossible for them to attempt to hold England strictly to international law on the seas. The English violations of international law in regard to neutral rights provoked the German submarine warfare in retaliation. This submarine warfare furnished the ostensible excuse for the American entry into the conflict, though Mr. Wilson had secretly conveyed to England his intention to enter the war on the side of the Entente nearly a year before the resumption of German submarine warfare if Germany would not agree to terms of peace which only a conquered state could be expected to accept. Colonel House was unquestionably a powerful factor in finally swinging Wilson for war.

"In estimating the order of guilt of the various countries we may safely say that the only direct and immediate responsibility for the World War falls upon France, Serbia and Russia, with the guilt about equally distributed. Next in order—far below France and Russia—would come Austria, for she never desired a general European war in 1914.

Finally, we should place Germany, England and Italy as tied for last place, all being opposed to war in the 1914 crisis. Probably the German public was somewhat more favorable to military activities than the English people, but, as we have shown, the Kaiser made much more strenuous efforts to preserve the peace of Europe in 1914 than did Sir Edward Grey.

"The really important aspect of the above material is not, of course, merely the satisfaction of our curiosity as to the historical facts regarding war origins, but the important bearing which these facts have on public opinion and international policy at the present time. As the prevailing European international policy is still based upon the assumption of the unique German responsibility for the war, it is evident, that the facts in the situation demand the repudiation of this programme and the adoption of a fair and constructive policy. The Dawes plan and the discussion which it has prompted, in common with most of the analyses of the reparations problem, rest upon altogether fallacious premises which invalidate alike the content of the proposal and the machinery of enforcement. The whole logical and juristic foundation of the notion of reparations for Germany and other defeated powers, in so far as it differs from the age-old policy of punitive levies on conquered peoples, is the assumption of the complete and unique responsibility of Germany for the origin of the World War and the misery, suffering and economic losses it entailed. This assumption is fully embodied in the Lansing report and in the provisions of the Treaty of Versailles relating to reparations. Even Poincaré was once incautious enough to admit that proof of divided responsibility for the outbreak of the great conflict carried with it a disappearance of the case for German reparations. The Dawes plan, and any current American and European agreements as to its enforcement, while immensely better than the Poincaré policy, are comparable to efforts to reduce the fine of a man, known by all informed persons to be innocent.

"What we need to do is to adopt a broad, constructive and farsighted policy. The guilt for the World War having been distributed, the expense of indemnifying the sufferers should not be thrown entirely on the least guilty nations. The United States might well use its undoubted financial power to induce France and England (the latter would probably gladly welcome the proposal) to forego all notion of any reparations from Germany and to adopt the programme of a mutual sharing with Germany of the burdens of reconstruction and rehabilitation. The United States could with great propriety indicate its good-will and intentions in the circumstances by cancelling the debts of the European powers on the above condition. Once England and France gave some such evidence of international honesty and decency, one of the chief obstacles and objections would be removed to the United States's joining the League of Nations. We may agree with Fabre-Luce that, though the wartime slogan that America and the Entente entered the war solely for the pur-

pose of ending all war was at the time pure hypocrisy, yet
we shall have lost both the war and the peace if we do not
take steps to make this constructive aspiration an achieved
reality. The beginnings of any such move must be found
in an appreciation of the facts concerning the origins of the
World War."

IV. Hon. John S. Ewart's Views

1. *Why France Entered the War*

In "The Roots and Causes of the Wars", 1914-1918, by
Honorable John S. Ewart, K. C., LL.D., etc., the learned
Canadian historian, whose monumental work of 1,200 pages
discloses a microscopic knowledge of the facts, appear a few
very condensed summaries, for example:

"Why did France enter the war? We may, therefore, say of the
reason which actuated France:

"1. It was not because of her interest in Serbia, or because of any
judgment as to the merits of the Serbian quarrel with Austro-
Hungary.

"2. It was not, simply, because of war-treaty with Russia.

"3. France entered the war because of 'the wound'; because *the
hour* of *revanche* had arrived; because she felt confident of her
military prowess; and because she deemed that her freedom from
future menace could be secured only by the abasement of Germany.

"4. In other words, France entered the war because urged thereto
by her own interests."

(Ewart 109)

2. *Did Germany Want War?*

"1. From the commencement of the diplomatizings prior to the war, Germany's chief effort was to 'localize' the war—that was, to confine it to a duel between Austro-Hungary and Serbia. Germany did not want a wider—a European war.

"2. When Serbia made humble reply to the Austro-Hungarian demands, the Kaiser declared that there was 'no longer any cause for war.' Thenceforward, until the mobilization of Russia against Germany, the German Chancellor did what he could to avoid all war.

"3. It was Germany's forty-three years of peace which had made possible her wonderful development. Her economic prosperity could not have been enhanced by war. Defeated or victorious, she would have suffered.

"4. For Germany there was no 'unredeemed territory'—no French Alsace-Lorraine; no Italian Trieste or Trentino; no Serbian Bosnia and Herzegovina; no Bulgarian Macedonia; no Turkish Thrace; no Roumanian Bessarabia, Transylvania, and Bukovina; no Russian Constantinople. Unlike other continental powers, Germany sought no territorial expansion in Europe, and the acquisition of territory elsewhere was less a desideratum in 1914 than some years previously."

(Ewart 94)

3. *"Why Did the United Kingdom Enter War?"*

"From what has been said, the following conclusions may safely be deduced:

"1. The merits of the quarrel between Austria-Hungary and Serbia were not a factor in the British determination to enter the war.

"2. There was no treaty obligation to defend Belgian neutrality. And Belgian neutrality could have been secured by the United Kingdom remaining neutral.

"3. An 'obligation of honor' to assist France existed. But it was evaded and, in effect, repudiated.

"4. Protection of 'small nationalities' was not a factor in the determination to enter the war.

"5. Nor was the hope of territorial aggrandisement.

"6. British self-interest was the reason for the form of the Belgian treaty in 1839; for Entente relations with France and Russia; for support of these Powers in various crises; for military and naval conventions with France; for naval arrangements with Russia; for Sir Edward Grey's letters to the French Ambassador of 22 November, 1912, and 2 August, 1914; and for entering upon the war.

"7. Embarrassed by previous denials of arrangements with France on the one hand, and by the German offer of Belgian neutrality on the other, Sir Edward Grey, in his speech of 3 August, 1914, asserted that nothing had been done which circumscribed the perfect liberty of the Government and the House to do as they pleased; left uncertain what he thought about the Belgian treaty; and omitted reference to the German offer of Belgian neutrality in consideration of British neutrality. The only reason for participation in the conflict which Sir Edward Grey clearly indicated was conservation of British interests."

(John S. Ewart, Roots and Causes of the Wars, page 198.)

V. The Conclusions of Mr. Lowes Dickinson

In his excellent work on *International Anarchy, 1904-1914,* the eminent English scholar, Mr. Lowes Dickinson, puts himself thoroughly on record as a member of the revisionist group of students of war guilt.

"Little Serbia stood on the verge of satisfying her national ambitions at the cost of the peoples and civilizations of three continents.

"For years the little State of Serbia had been undermining the Austrian Empire. . . What was the Empire to do in self-defense? One can conceive a world in which Austria would not have wished to hold down a nationality against its will. But that would not be the world of history, past or present. Never has an empire resigned before the disruptive forces of nationality. Always it has fought. And I do not believe that there was a State in existence that would not, under similar circumstances, have determined, as Austria did, to finish the menace, once for all, by war. . . With every year that passed the Austrian position would get worse and the Serbian better. So at least the Austrians thought, and not without reason. They took their risk according to the usual canons in such matters. They may be accused of miscalculation, but I do not see that they can be accused of wrong by any one who accepts now, or who accepted then, the principles which have always dictated the policy of States. German diplomacy was cumbersome, stupid, and dishonest. Granted, it was! But German policy was such as any State would have adopted in her position. The Powers of the Entente say that the offense was Germany's backing of Austria. Germans say that the offense was Russia's backing of Serbia. On that point, really, the whole controversy turns. To my mind the German position is the more reasonable.

"Why was the war not localized, as Austria and Germany intended and desired? There is only one answer to this: because Russia did not choose to allow it. Why not? . . . The answer is that she wanted Constantinople and the Straits; that she wanted access to the Mediterranean; that she wanted extension of territory and influence; that she had a 'historic mission'; that she must make herself secure; in short, the whole farrago of superstitions that dominate all States under the conditions of the armed anarchy. . . France entered for the sake of the balance of power and to recover Alsace-Lorraine; and her technical success in waiting till the declaration of war came from Germany does not alter the position. It had been known for at least two years past, it was reaffirmed more than once during the crisis that, if Germany came in against Russia, France would come in against Germany. . . At any rate, since 1912 France would have entered when Russia did. And does any one who has perused the previous chapters, and who realizes the state of Europe, believe that Russia would not have started the war a year or two later? . . . And England? . . . She had military and naval commitments to France which were like a suction-pipe to draw her, whether she would or no, into the war. And that approximation to the other two powers of the Entente was made for no other reason than the maintenance of the balance of power. We had become more afraid of Germany than of our traditional enemies, France and Russia. After all of our commitments to France it would have been base to desert her. Agreed! But what were the objects for which those commitments were made? Our own power, our own empire, our own security."

VI. THE FOURTEEN PLEDGES AND THE TREATY OF VERSAILLES

In the newly discovered light of the disclosures that the German leaders did not will the World War; that they were opposed to the World War; that the World War was desired by the Russian leaders and brought about by them, it seems worth while to consider the conditions upon which the German people surrendered and agreed to the Armistice on November 11, 1918.

The German people surrendered on the promises made to them through the President of the United States, acting as a spokesman of the Entente Allies. These promises were made in writing, and after nine days' discussion at the Palace of the Trianon at Versailles, near Paris, they were accepted in writing by the representatives of Great Britain, France, Italy, Belgium, Japan and the United States. These pledges made to the German people upon which they agreed to lay down their arms and upon which the Emperor of

Germany resigned and left Germany, are commonly known as the Fourteen Points. The written agreement stipulates on behalf of the Entente Allies:

"Their willingness to make peace with the Government of Germany on the terms of peace laid down in the President's address to Congress in January, 1918, and the principles of settlement enunciated in his subsequent addresses."

These pledges made to the German people through the President of the United States, on behalf of the Allies, under this written agreement promised:

No punitive damages; no annexations, no indemnities; no selfish economic combinations; no special or separate interest of any single nation or any group of nations as a basis of any part of the settlement.

The consent of all nations to be governed in their conduct toward each other by the same principles of honor and of respect for the common law of civilized society that governs the individual citizens of all modern states in their relations with one another.

The destruction of any arbitrary power in rule that can separately, secretly and of its own single choice disturb the peace of the world.

The right to live on equal terms of liberty and safety; a place of equality among the peoples of the earth.

The protection of territorial integrity and political independence.

The impartial adjustment of colonial claims; the elimination of economic powers; equality of trade. The end of secret diplomacy.

The pledges are as binding on the conscience of mankind today as they were when they were written and signed on the 4th of November, 1918; as they were on the 11th day of November, 1918, when the Germans surrendered in pursuance of these pledges.

The Treaty of Versailles violated these pledges, and put the United States in the attitude of having betrayed the German people through the President of the United States. This miscarriage of justice was due to the violent passions of war and to a profound misconception of its origin. It was the Russian leaders that willed and caused this war. The Germans were believed the guilty parties and the treaty was intended to punish them.

The Versailles Treaty made under such blinding prejudice and signed by the officials of the German people under violent protest at the point of the bayonet, has no legal or moral binding force. The welfare of the world, the reconciliation of the peoples of Europe require the elimination of Articles 227 and 231, inclusive, and that this treaty should be so modified as to make amends to the German people for the wrongs done them by the Treaty of Versailles.

Article 227 recites:

"The Allied and Associated Powers publicly arraign William II, of Hohenzollern, formerly German Emperor, for a supreme offense against international morality and the sanctity of treaties," and solemnly provides for his trial. The Allied and Associated Powers did not try William II for the excellent reason that if they had done so, certain former very distinguished leaders of the Entente Allies would have been shown to be responsible for the war and thus themselves guilty—

"of a supreme offense against international morality and the sanctity of treaties."

For the most part the Entente leaders were sincere in the belief that William II was responsible. A few of them in very high places knew that the charge was false. The leaders of the United States had no means of knowing it. The shallow pretense offered to the world as the reason for not trying William II was that the good Wilhelmina, Queen of Holland, would not permit them to do so. This excuse is ludicrous, and should not deceive a person of any mentality whatever. The Entente had all the military power in the world and could have compelled Holland to deliver William II. The reason is obvious why it was not done.

The charge of Article 231 that the war was imposed on the Allies and Associated Governments by the aggression of Germany and her allies is also entirely untrue, as the official records now exposed to view overwhelmingly demonstrate. The historians who have studied this record are in agreement with regard to the vital facts.

Article 231 should be eliminated.

First—Because it is untrue.

Second—Because the acceptance of this article by Germany was at the point of the bayonet, threatening the German people with destruction. Such a confession is morally worthless, and without binding force.

Third—Besides being false and worthless, it remains a subject of profound international irritation, building up among the German people a dangerous spirit of ultimate revenge, and *making it impossible for them to believe in the integrity of the Entente leadership.*

The establishment of international understanding and international good will requires only common honesty and common sense.

VII. A French Appeal to Conscience

Under this heading, first signed by *one hundred distinguished French historians, authors, men of letters, including five distinguished French Generals* who had fought in the war, and since by increasing numbers, appears the following intelligent proposal from Paris, France, looking to the moral disarmament of Europe:

"Only a misunderstanding keeps the world from peace, and perpetuates between the former belligerents, and particularly between France and Germany, that spirit of war which is born fatally from a sense of injustice inseparable from the instinct of revenge.

"German opinion only submits with profound revolt to Articles 227 to 230, and to Article 231 of the Treaty of Versailles, of which this is the tenor:

" 'The Allied and Associated Governments declare and Germany acknowledges that Germany and its allies are responsible for having caused them all the loss and damage endured by the Allied and Associated Governments and their nationals in consequence of the war which was imposed on them by the aggression of Germany and of its allies.'

"It is not against the material facts of reparation that the German nation raises its protest. It recognizes the necessity of reparation. It bowed to the rule of international law.

"That which it does not accept is that there has been snatched from it by force a confession against which, before as after its signature, it has not ceased to protest, and where it saw proclaimed to the world its one-sided culpability as to the origin and therefore as to the responsibility of the war.

"France on the other side holds to the doctrine that the aggression materialized by the invasion of Belgium. Such is the situation full of danger which should at all costs be cleared up. First, the question at bottom.

"It is impossible to prejudge that question here. That immense process of judgment in which all humanity is interested can only be argued, in the complex detail of its causes, when all the archives are open and before a high supranational court. Let us nevertheless consider a preliminary proposition. It is clear that the official documents witness that Article 231 was only extorted from Germany by violence and under the threat of recommencing war to the point of complete ruin. Could we give the force of right to that proceeding so unworthy of civilization, after having declared that we were carrying on a war of right against might? The day of summary judgments without appeal is passed. It is as unfair to condemn a people to dishonor without a hearing as it is an individual to death. We Frenchmen, jealous of the honor of our country, and believing also firmly that every violation of justice brings with it future catastrophe, are unwilling to face the reproach of a violation of the very principles which we ourselves have been proclaiming. Even if there cannot be in the meantime the question of a material change in the Treaty, which belongs alone to time and the society of nations, and we can no longer act with regard to the regulation of reparations fixed by the Convention of London, August, 1924, yet there rests at least upon our good will a duty to see that the Treaty shall not impose greater weight upon the unstable equilibrium in which we are living.

"There is no security in the future if men do not proceed first toward moral disarmament, without which there never will be material disarmament possible. Article 231 should be modified in a sense acceptable to all, as well there should be abrogated Articles 227 to 230 (title: Sanctions), which, encouraging hate with its reprisals, are not less injurious to the definite re-establishment of peace.

"We are at the cross-roads. It is necessary to choose. On the one side all the evils of war perpetuated by the spirit of revenge; on the other, sincere reconciliation and productive labor. We invite all those who hold in their hearts love of justice and of truth, all those who ardently desire that their children should have a future free from war, to join their efforts with ours. The Nationalists of Germany must not misunderstand us. Here is no proof of weakness—only an evidence of French sense of right; a step toward human solidarity. The Germany of Goethe will comprehend it.

"European civilization is risking in these tragic days its entire future. It is lost if the butchery recommences."

Victor Margueritte, in his foreword to the Appeal to Conscience, declares that Germany from the beginning of the negotiations to 1919 has never admitted the charge of having caused the war, as Margueritte calls it "The Brand of the Red Hot Iron". He says:

"The White Book, published by M. Mennevée, bears testimony in the most impressive fashion. The documents, the proofs are there; the act of accusation, a tissue of inexactitudes; the solemn protest of Brockdorff-Rantzau; the sober concluding memoir of Germany fortified with a mass of proof; the feeble response of the Allies; * * * Finally, the ultimatum of Clemenceau giving five days for acceptance under penalty of a rupture of the Armistice and recommencement of the war.

"One cannot read what follows without sadness and without shame; the vehement supplication of the President of the Ministry of the Empire; the brutal refusal of delay by Clemenceau; the Allied troops ready to pass the Rhine, while the assembly of Weimar was deliberating; the final demand for delay while in place of the Minister of Resistance, a Minister of Capitulation succeeded; the incriminating summary cutting short everything up to the last cry thrown back by the head of the German delegation. It was a moving scene and worthy of the cry which burst forth from Haniel as an 'unheard of injustice' in which he submitted himself at the same time that he flayed the act of violence against the honor of his people.

"Since that time by the voice of its chancellors, of its parliament, of its writers, Germany has not ceased to protest. It has seemed to me, and to a certain number of free spirits who have thought as I do, that we could no longer admit that France should close its eyes and its ears. Involuntary ignorance is an excuse, but wilful ignorance is more than a fault. It is a stupidity and an inexplicable dishonor."

VIII. British Appeal to Conscience

In December, 1925, the following petition was signed by many prominent Englishmen, and presented to the British Government. Among the signatures were many professors of history, etc., such as Professor Raymond Beazley, of Birmingham University; G. Lowes Dickinson, author of "International Anarchy", Kings College, Cambridge; Professor J. J. Findley, Manchester University; Professor H. Fleure, of University of Wales; Professor A. J. Grant, of Leeds University; Professor J. H. Muirhead, of Birmingham University; Professor Gilbert Murray, of Oxford University; Professor A. F. Pollard, University of London; Professor

Percy M. Roxby, of Liverpool University; Professor Frederick Sonny, of the University of Oxford; the Right Reverend the Bishop of Birmingham; the Right Reverend the Bishop of Manchester; G. Bernard Shaw; H. G. Wells; Lady Gladstone; the notable historian G. P. Gooch; John Maynard Keynes; Lascelles Abercrombie; Professor Alexander, of Manchester, and others.

MANIFESTO

"Deeply moved by the manifesto signed by over one hundred French men and women of distinction, and published in L'Ere Nouvelle, on July 9, 1925, we undersigned British citizens declare ourselves in cordial agreement with its plea that the Treaty of Versailles should be amended in two points:

"(1) Article 231 attributes the origin of the war simply to 'the aggression of Germany and her Allies.' Without at this time expressing any opinion or withdrawing any opinion which we have previously expressed as to the policies of the late Imperial German Government, we regard it as an improper and dangerous precedent, that the victors in a war should thus pronounce judgment on the vanquished. Such judgment, if it is to have any legal or moral authority, should be pronounced by an impartial court after careful study of all the evidence.

"(2) Articles 227 to 230 dealing with offences against 'international morality and the sanctity of treaties' or 'violation of the laws and customs of war,' provide that any Germans guilty of such crimes shall be tried and punished by courts set up by their enemies, but make no provision either for the creation of an impartial court or for the trial and punishment of criminals who are not German. The injustice of this cannot be disputed.

"We regard these articles, which were forcibly imposed upon a defeated nation under the most terrible threats, as having expressed a state of mind in the Allied and Associated Powers, which has now largely passed away. We believe that they are manifestly unjust and constitute a grave obstacle to international understanding. Consequently we urge the governments concerned either to amend these Articles with no further delay or, if amendment of the treaty prove too long and cumbrous a proceeding, to announce severally their intention to disregard them."

IX. THE MANIA OF WAR

At 7 P. M. on Saturday, August 1, 1914, the German Ambassador, Portalés, notified Sazonoff, the Minister of Foreign Affairs of Russia, that the Emperor of Germany, after his strenuous and unavailing efforts for peace, accepted the challenge of Russia, and considered himself at war with Russia, because the Russian acts threatened Germany so dangerously that the safety of Germany no longer permitted him to disregard these acts, which he regarded as a determined will to war.

Instantly this communication was telegraphed and telephoned all over Europe as a declaration of war by Germany. The predetermined war was officially recognized as existing. The war was officially a fact. The people, the men and women and youth of Europe, as well as the officials, civil, military and naval, became mad with the passion of war.

The Russian people damned the German people with every execration for wilfully declaring war on them, and during August, when hundreds of thousands of men were killed in battle in East-Prussia and in Belgium and in France, the people of Belgium and the people of France cursed the Germans and gave them derisive names as Huns and Boches, and made the German name increasingly detestable by terrible stories of unspeakable brutality and of hideous atrocity. The German people, in like manner, cursed from the bottom of their souls the Russians who struck Eastern Germany with 800,000 invading troops before the Germans could collect themselves for defense, and the English, whom they consigned to divine wrath. This mania of war which justified mass slaughter broke down the moral standards even in the highest places. Nothing was too bad to say of the enemy. It became a merit to charge them with every conceivable crime, and as the homes of France and Germany received the news of the deaths and terrible wounds of their best beloved sons, this bitterness and hate increased to the extremest depth of human passion.

Of course there were barbarities and atrocities. The German, Russian, French and other armies all developed soldiers who committed atrocities.

War did not respect life nor property nor the pursuit of happiness, nor the Ten Commandments. The moral and ethical standards of men became almost completely obscured. John Morley has well said: "That is the worst of war; it ostracises, demoralizes, brutalizes reason." The highest officials employed experts to carry on propaganda to stimulate their own people by exciting their animosities against the enemies. Even in America our people became so infuriated by this propaganda that in many cases the simplest elements of common sense vanished. Many a faithful citizen of German origin was ostracised and ill-treated without evidence against him during the War. His German name sufficed for proof, although he may have been born in America and had lived a useful, upright life as a good American citizen and his loyalty perfect.

The world went mad, and while the Fourteen Points, after nine days' discussion at Versailles, were solemnly agreed to and signed by the representatives of Great Britain, France, Italy, Belgium, Japan, and the United States, on November 4, 1918, the controlling representatives of France, Italy, Belgium and Great Britain, under the mania of war, framed the Versailles Treaty in flat violation of many of these vital promises, and Article 231 even compelled the German Republic to confess complete responsibility for having imposed the war on the Allies. The German leaders vehemently, strenuously, pathetically protested against this Article. The Allies, led by Clemenceau, compelled them to sign the Treaty at the point of the bayonet when the German people were disarmed.

The mania of war in June, 1919, had not been abated. The fury growing out of the terrific slaughter was dominant. The blood and dust of battle were still in the eyes of the leaders. They could not clearly see. Doubtless the majority of these leaders, who did not then know, and who did not then have any opportunity of knowing the truth, which we now know, sincerely believed the German government had been exclusively responsible for the war.

Seven years have passed, and in that time all the Russian records have been fully exposed to view, and have disclosed to the world the selfish Imperial Russian conspiracy against Germany and against Europe.

Isvolski and Sazonoff and Sukhomlinoff thought but little of the consequences to the common soldiers of Russia, much less the common soldiers of France and Germany. They had their eager eyes fixed on the glory of the Imperial Russian dynasty. They were going to control Constantinople and the Dardanelles. They were going to exercise overlordship of the Balkan Slav States. They were going to appropriate the eastern portion of Austria and Germany, have ice free ports on the Baltic and access to the Adriatic.

Man proposes; God disposes.

This Imperial Conspiracy caused the killing and wounding of 37,000,000 of men—Russians, French, Germans and people from the ends of the earth. It caused other millions of men to die without record and vanish. It caused millions of women and children to die unrecorded. It devastated Europe. It broke down the moral standards of mankind throughout the world. The war was followed by waves of epidemic diseases and crime, sweeping the world from one end to the other. Boys and girls were corrupted. The ancient standards of the sacred rights of private property vanished from Eastern Europe, and were seriously weakened throughout all Europe. All the Russian Imperialists, almost without exception, met with death, banishment, poverty or distress. They paid a terrible penalty for their folly. The Czar and all of his family were murdered and with the destruction of the power of the Romanoffs came the destruction also of the Imperial house of the Hohenzollerns and Hapsburgs. But the people of the world, especially of France and Germany, should remember that they were all alike the victims of the ambition, vanity, folly of human leadership, and that if the world had been controlled by educated Democracies, the opinion of the intelligence of mankind based on the moderate judgment of the majorities in the various nations, would never have led to the slaughter of the youth of the world.

"All of the people *know more* than some of the people." (Lincoln.)

Lincoln wisely prayed that government of the people, by the people, for the people should not perish from the earth. The Imperial Russian conspiracy has greatly advanced government by the people, and *the greatest need of the world now is that government by the people should be strenuously supplemented by education of the people*. The greatest of all teachers said:

"Ye shall know the truth, and the truth shall make you free."

X. CONCLUSION

From these records, of which only vital portions have been presented, it is absolutely clear:

First—That the common people of Russia, France, and Germany desired peace and did not wish war, but that a very few men in France and the Imperialists of Russia planned in 1892 to arrange for ultimate war on Germany.

Second—That they prepared for it during twenty years, during which by subsidizing the French Press with Russian money, borrowed from the French, and expended under the French Minister of Foreign Affairs, the French common people were induced to buy $7,000,000,000 of Russian bonds, which were employed in building up a huge Russian army, to manufacture supplies of heavy and light artillery and munitions of war, to double-track their railways to the German border, for the purpose of carrying out the military conventions of making offensive war on Germany.

Third—That in order to make a certainty of success in this gigantic conspiracy, Germany was encircled with a series of treaties or understandings between Russia and France; between Russia and Roumania; Russia and Bulgaria; Russia and Serbia, and gentlemen's agreements between Russia and Italy; Russia and Great Britain; France and Great Britain; France and Belgium, so that Germany was completely surrounded on land and sea.

Fourth—That as part of this strategy to throw the moral influence of the world against Germany, Germany was made to appear as guilty of having started the war. This was done by mobilizing the troops of Russia through a general mobilization order (the military equivalent of a declaration of war by Russia, but not so understood by the public), which called to the Russian colors 14,000,000 men, and concentrated such masses of Russian troops against the German border that the military leaders of Germany as a military necessity, had no option whatever, except to recognize what was a fact, "a state of war existing." This was only done on August 1, 1914, at 7 P. M., after the Russian mobilization had been in progress for approximately eight days.

Fifth—That immediately Germany took this official step, desired by the conspirators, Germany was blockaded by land and sea, and the most gigantic propaganda the world had ever known was begun by the Entente Allies to prove to the world that the German leaders were solely responsible for the war; that the German purpose was to conquer Europe and to become the military dictator of the world; that the Germans were waging war with fiendish cruelty.

The conspiracy of the Russian and French leaders succeeded completely. All the world believed Germany guilty, and when the Treaty of Versailles was written in June, 1919, the German Government was compelled by military force to confess that Germany had imposed the war on the Allies.

Such a confession so extorted has in history no equal in the magnitude of its injustice. This confession of guilt should be removed, and the world brought back to understanding, truth and good will.

America has keenly felt the terrible war losses which afflicted all our communities through the death and wounding of our young men, through social, business and financial disturbances, and through the taxation of war.

We have sympathized with the French people, whose country was invaded, who suffered gigantic loss of the best young men of France, and who suffered ruinous property losses because of war and are still feeling its evil consequences. We have forgiven them a large part of the debt due us.

We have sympathized with the British people who have suffered in the same way and have been in like manner generous to them.

America has made large contributions to relieve the affliction of Belgium, whose people were the innocent victims of this terrible struggle.

We have sympathized with the Russian people, who suffered the greatest loss of any of the nations in human life and in the breaking down of the moral and social standards of life. We sent millions to relieve them of famine.

In view of the recorded proof that the German people and even the German leaders did not will this war, but were the victims of a conspiracy of the Russian Imperial power, *is it not reasonable that the Christian world should feel some sense of sympathy for the women and children and even for the men of Germany?*

Nearly 8,000,000 German soldiers were killed or wounded. The German people suffered severely from famine, which destroyed life on a large scale. They had to go through complete national bankruptcy. Not only were they taxed to the limit of their capacity, but all their savings accounts measured in marks were reduced to zero. The bank balances

of the middle class vanished for like reason. All the bonds
they held in German companies, or which had been issued
by the States and Municipalities of Germany, or given by
private persons, became completely worthless because of
the destruction of the mark. All of their insurance policies
became valueless. Thousands of middle class Germans committed suicide in despair.

The German people have been through every suffering
people could endure, and they were innocent of evil intent.

Even today, 1,500,000 of them are unemployed (March,
1927).

*Does not the world owe them some sympathy? Was ever
a great civilized people more wronged in the esteem and respect of the world than the Germans? Is the frightful
tragedy unjustly visited upon them nothing to us?*

In America we have 20,000,000 people who are directly
descended from the German stock. These peaceful, industrious, home-loving descendants of German ancestry deserve
well of America. Their good name and their affections are
involved in the honor of the German name.

America, like the balance of the world, swept away by the
rage of war, largely imagined the Germans to be criminal;
that they had deliberately brought on this war for the purpose of conquering the whole world. Only the mania of
war could have made such a belief possible, and not until
five years after the war was it discovered through disclosures
of the secret records of Russia that we had been terribly
misled.

The establishment of the truth as to the origin of the World War is vital to a reconciliation of the people of Europe, to their moral disarmament, to their future peace and happiness. It is vital to the future interest of America that Europe and the world should be at peace and prosperous.

America was nevertheless gravely deceived by European propaganda as to the origin and the purposes of the World War and is now being subjected to a similar propaganda for the cancellation of the war debts. Never was it more important to the people of the United States than to consider very soberly at this time the advice of George Washington in his farewell address.

The Father of our country wisely and nobly said:

"Observe good faith and justice towards all nations; cultivate peace and harmony with all." . . . "Nothing is more essential than that permanent, inveterate antipathies against particular nations and passionate attachments for others should be excluded; and that, in place of them, just and amicable feelings towards all should be cultivated." . . .

"Antipathy in one nation against another, disposes each more readily to offer insult and injury, to lay hold of slight causes of umbrage, and to be haughty and intractable when accidental or trifling occasions of dispute occur. Hence, frequent collisions, obstinate, envenomed and bloody contests." . . .

"So likewise, a passionate attachment of one nation for another produces a variety of evils. Sympathy for the favorite nation, facilitating the illusion of an imaginary common interest, in cases where no real common interest exists, and infusing into one the enmities of the other, betrays the former into a participation in the quarrels and wars of the latter, without adequate inducements or justification. It leads also to concession, to the favorite nation, of privilege denied to others, which is apt doubly to injure the nation making the concessions, by unnecessarily parting with what ought to have been retained, and by exciting jealousy, ill-will, and a disposition to retaliate in the parties from whom equal privileges are withheld; and it gives to ambitious, corrupted or deluded citizens who devote themselves to the favorite nation, facility to betray or sacrifice the interests of their own country, without odium, sometimes even with popularity; gilding with the appearances of a virtuous sense of obligation, a commendable deference for public opinion or a laudable zeal for the public good, the base or foolish compliances of ambition, corruption, or infatuation."

XI. BIBLIOGRAPHY
OFFICIAL DOCUMENTS

Evidence and historical works relating to the Russian conspiracy.
1. LA GUERRE EUROPÉENE (Livre Jaune, 1914.)
2. LES AFFAIRES FRANCO-BALKANIQUES, 3 vols. (Livre Jaune, 1922).
3. L'ALLIANCE FRANCO-RUSSE (Livre Jaune, 1918).
4. LES ACCORDS FRANCO-ITALIENS (Livre Jaune, 1920).
5. LIVRE BLEU ANGLAIS (1914).
6. LIVRE ORANGE RUSSE (1914).
7. LIVRE BLANC ALLEMAND (1914).
8. LIVRE BLANC ALLEMAND (1919), publié par R. Mennevée.
9. LES DOCUMENTS ALLEMANDS, rassemblés par Kautsky, Montgelas et Schucking, 4 vols. 1922, traduction de C. Jordan.
10. PIÈCES DIPLOMATIQUES. Supplément et additions au Livre Rouge Austro-Hongrois. 3 vols. 1922, traduction de C. Jordan.

11. ENTENTE DIPLOMACY AND THE WORLD. Benno von Siebert; Knickerbocker Press, New York. *The Secret Dispatches of the Russian London Embassy.*
12. UN LIVRE NOIR (Russian Archives), 2 volumes. René Marchand; Librairie du Travail, Paris. *The Secret Dispatches of the Russian Embassy at Paris.*
13. THE SECRET TREATIES. F. Seymour Cocks.
14. OUTBREAK OF THE WORLD WAR. German documents collected by Karl Kautsky and edited by Max Montgelas and Walther Shucking. 688 pp. Karl Kautsky. New York, 1924.
15. INTRODUCTION AUX TABLEAUX D'HISTOIRE COMPARÉE. C. Appuhn et P. Renouvin.
16. TABLEAUX D'HISTOIRE COMPARÉE ET MÉMOIRES. Guillaume II.
17. LES DOCUMENTS BELGES.
18. LES DOCUMENTS POLITIQUES, DIPLOMATIQUES ET FINANCIERS. R. Mennevée.

FRENCH AUTHORS

19. LA MOBILISATION RUSSE EN 1914. General Dobrorolsky.
20. THE ORIGINS OF THE WAR. 230 pp. Raymond Poincaré. London, 1922.
21. LES RESPONSABILITÉS DE LA GUERRE. George Demartial.
22. CONSIDERATIONS SUR LES RESPONSABILITÉS DE LA GUERRE. Gustav Dupin.
23. POINCARÉ A-T-IL VOULU LA GUERRE? Gouttenoiro de Toury.
24. SECRET DOCUMENTS OF THE ARCHIVES OF THE MINISTER OF FOREIGN AFFAIRS OF RUSSIA. Emile Laloy.
25. LA VICTOIRE (Now translated, Knopf). *The Limitations of Victory.* 428 pp. A. Fabre-Luce. Paris, 1924.
26. LES CRIMINELS. 356 pp. Victor Margueritte. Paris, 1925.
27. LES PREUVES. *Le Crime de Droit Commun. Le Crime Diplomatique.* 340 pp. Mathias Morhardt. Paris, 1924.
28. LA RUSSIE DES TSARS PENDANT LA GRANDE GUERRE. 3 vols. Maurice Paleologue. Paris, 1922.
29. LES RESPONSABLES DE LA GUERRE. 520 pp. Alfred Pévet. Paris, 1921.
30. A L'ORIGINE DU MENSONGE. Lazare.
31. LES ORIGINES IMMÉDIATE DE LA GUERRE. P. Renouvin.
32. LES ORIGINES ET LES RESPONSABILITÉS DE LA GRANDE GUERRE. P. Renouvin et G. Pages.
33. HISTOIRE POPULAIRE DE LA GUERRE DE 1914-19. 3 vols. Ernest Renauld.
34. VERS LA VERITÉ. Gustav Dupin.

35. LA GUERRE INFERNALE. Gustav Dupin.
36. CONSIDERATIONS SUR LES RESPONSABILITÉS. Gustav Dupin.
37. JUILLET 1914, etc. Gustav Dupin.
38. GEORGE LOUIS. Ernest Judet.
39. COMMENT ON MOBILIZA LES CONSCIENCES. G. Demartial.
40. AGADIR. J. Caillaux.
41. OÙ VA LA FRANCE? J. Caillaux.
42. OÙ VA L'EUROPE? J. Caillaux.
43. TROIS ANS DE DIPLOMATIE SECRÈTE. Colonel Converset.
44. CHACUN SON TOUR. Charles Humbert.
45. LA PAIX MALPROPRE. Alcide Ebray.

RUSSIAN AUTHORS

46. DOCUMENTS HISTORIQUES DES ALLIES CONTRA LA RUSSIE—by 14
     Russian Generals and Admirals.
47. MÉMOIRES. Comte Witte.
48. RECOLLECTIONS OF A FOREIGN MINISTER. Isvolski; Doubleday,
     Page & Co., New York.
          [See Numbers 11 and 12 above.]

SERBIAN AUTHOR

49. LES CAUSES DE LA GUERRE. Dr. M. Boghitchevitch.

ENGLISH AUTHORS

50. A REVISION OF THE TREATY. J. M. Keynes; Harcourt, Brace &
     Co., New York.
51. TEN YEARS OF SECRET DIPLOMACY. E. D. Morel; National Labor
     Press, Manchester.
52. PREWAR DIPLOMACY, 1919. E. D. Morel.
53. DIPLOMATIC GENESIS OF WAR. E. D. Morel.
54. TRUTH AND THE WAR. E. D. Morel.
55. THE SECRET HISTORY OF A GREAT BETRAYAL. E. D. Morel.
56. DIPLOMACY REVEALED. E. D. Morel.
57. INTERNATIONAL ANARCHY. G. L. Dickinson.
58. THE CAUSES OF INTERNATIONAL WAR. G. L. Dickinson; Har-
     court, Brace & Howe, New York.
59. HOW DIPLOMATS MAKE WAR. Francis Neilson; B. W. Huebsch,
     New York.
60. MY MISSION TO RUSSIA AND OTHER DIPLOMATIC MEMOIRS.
     2 vols. Sir George Buchanan. London, 1923.
61. A HISTORY OF MODERN EUROPE, 1878-1920. 728 pp. G. P. Gooch.
     New York, 1923.

GERMAN AUTHORS

62. THE FALSIFICATION OF THE RUSSIAN ORANGE BOOK. Baron von Romberg; B. W. Huebsch, New York.
63. SUR LA QUESTION DES RESPONSABILITÉS. Count Montgelas.
64. COMMENT S'EST DECLANCHÉE LA GUERRE MONDIALE. Karl Kautsky.
65. THE CASE FOR THE CENTRAL POWERS. 255 pp. Max Montgelas. New York, 1925.
66. ISVOLSKI AND THE WORLD WAR. Stieve.
67. REFLECTIONS OF THE WORLD WAR. Bethmann-Hollweg; Thornton, Butterworth, London.

AMERICAN AUTHORS

68. LET FRANCE EXPLAIN. Bausman; Allen & Unwin, London.
69. LEX TALIONIS. Hills; Fleet, McGinley Co., Baltimore.
70. THE MYTH OF A GUILTY NATION. Nock; B. W. Huebsch, New York.
71. ECONOMIC IMPERIALISM. Leonard Wolk; Harcourt, Brace & Howe, New York.
72. NEW LIGHT ON THE ORIGINS OF THE WORLD WAR, in *American Historical Review,* July, 1920; October, 1920; January, 1921. Sidney B. Fay.
73. SERBIA'S RESPONSIBILITY FOR THE WORLD WAR, in *New York Times Current History Magazine,* October, 1925. Sidney B. Fay.
74. THE BLACK HAND PLOT THAT LED TO THE WORLD WAR, in *New York Times Current History Magazine,* November, 1925. Sidney B. Fay.
75. GENESIS OF THE WORLD WAR. Prof. H. E. Barnes; A. A. Knopf, N. Y.
76. THE VERDICT OF HISTORY; E. F. Henderson. THE CASE OF SIR EDWARD GRAY; Monadnock, N. H., 1924.

CANADIAN AUTHOR

77. JOHN S. EWART. THE ROOTS AND CAUSES OF THE WARS. 2 vols. New York, 1925.

ITALIAN AUTHOR

78. L'EUROPE SANS PAIX, etc., etc. Francesco Nitti.